It's All in Your Head

Also by Stephen M. Pollan and Mark Levine

Fire Your Boss

Second Acts

Die Broke

Live Rich

The Die Broke Complete Book of Money

The Die Broke Financial Problem Solver

By Stephen M. Pollan
and Mark Levine

BEST-SELLING AUTHORS OF
SECOND ACTS AND *DIE BROKE*

Collins

An Imprint of HarperCollins*Publishers*

It's All in Your Head

(Thinking Your Way to Happiness)

The

8 Essential Secrets

to Leading a Life

Without Regrets

DESIGNED BY NICOLA FERGUSON

ISBN-13: 978-0-06-075999-5
ISBN-10: 0-06-075999-2

To my grandchildren.
—Stephen Pollan

To Rocky and Winston.
—Mark Levine

MORAL

Happiness is a how, not a what; a talent,
not an object.

—HERMANN HESSE

Contents

Acknowledgments

A book like this draws not only on people with whom we've spoken, but on books we've read, movies and television shows we've watched, music we've heard, and art we've seen. To come up with a comprehensive list of all the sources and influences that helped us write this book is, as a result, impossible. Instead we're forced to highlight only a handful of influences. We apologize, in advance to all those we've left out.

Thanks to the friends, family, and clients who allowed us to draw on the stories of their lives as examples in this book.

Thanks to David Allen, Saint Augustine, Hannah Arendt, Marcus Aurelius, Honoré de Balzac, John Barrymore, Walter Benjamin, Ambrose Bierce, Jorge Luis Borges, Urie Bronfenbrenner, Frank Buchman, Frances Burney, Samuel Butler, Julius Caesar, Albert Camus, Angela Carter, Miguel de Cervantes, Martin Charnin, Joseph Conrad, Mason Cooley, Nathaniel Cotton, Faye J. Crosby, Robertson Davies, Charles Dickens, Diogenes, Leo Durocher, Ralph Waldo Emerson, Epictetus, Gustave Flaubert, Anne Frank, Baltasar Gracián, Robert Grudin, Hermann Hesse, Eric Hoffer, Oliver Wendell

Holmes Sr., Thomas Henry Huxley, Eugène Ionesco, William James, Susan Jeffers, Thomas Jefferson, Janis Joplin, Franz Kafka, Yoshida Kenkō, Ernest Kurtz, Philip Larkin, D. H. Lawrence, Henry Wadsworth Longfellow, Dominic Maruca, Margaret Mead, Thomas Moore, O. Herbert Mowrer, Fridtjof Nansen, John Henry Cardinal Newman, Blaise Pascal, Alastair Reed, François, Duc de La Rochefoucauld, Jean Rostand, Wendy Coppedge Sandford, Arthur Schopenhauer, George Bernard Shaw, Baruch Spinoza, Publius Syrus, Henry David Thoreau, Roderick Thorp, Mark Twain, Walt Whitman, Oscar Wilde, Thornton Wilder, Frank Lloyd Wright, Steven Wright, and Stefan Zweig for lending us their words of wisdom.

Thanks to Steve Hanselman for helping to inspire this book.

Thanks to Joe Tessitore, Libby Jordan, Herb Schaffner, Knox Huston, Paul Olsewski, and Keith Pfeffer of Collins for their vision and encouragement throughout the project. In fact, we'd like to thank everyone at HarperCollins. For years we talked about finding a home with a publisher. Thanks to the extraordinary people at HarperCollins, past and present, we've now had a happy home on 53rd Street for seven years and as many books.

Thanks to our agent, Stuart Krichevsky, and Shana Cohen and Elizabeth Coen of the Stuart Krichevsky Literary Agency for their unflinching help and support. We're always told how rare it is for authors to have as close and lasting a relationship to an agent as we have with Stuart. That's a testimony to his skill, vision, humor, and above all, patience.

Thanks to our wives, Corky Pollan and Deirdre Martin Levine, for their understanding and love.

PROLOGUE

A Hindu legend says we were all once gods. But eventually we abused our powers. Brahma, the chief god, decided to punish us by taking away our divinity. Brahma called a meeting of the other chief gods to figure out where to hide our holiness. One god suggested hiding it deep beneath the earth. "No," Brahma said, "man will just figure out a way to tunnel miles below the surface." Another god suggested hiding our holiness at the bottom of the ocean. "No," Brahma responded, "man will just learn how to dive to the seabed." A third god came up with the idea of placing our divinity on top of a towering mountain. "No," Brahma said, "man will just climb every tall mountain on the planet until he finds it." Stumped, the other gods told Brahma they gave up—there didn't seem to be any place to hide our holiness and keep it out of our reach. "Wait," Brahma said with a smile. "I've got it. We'll hide man's holiness deep within himself—he'll never think to look for it there." Since then, we've spent ages digging below the earth, diving to the sea floor, and climbing tall mountains, looking for something that's already within us.

It's All in
Your Head

(1)

IT'S ALL IN YOUR HEAD

The search for happiness is one of the chief sources of unhappiness.
—*Eric Hoffer*

Are there times you feel you're missing the one or two crucial ingredients you need to be happy? Maybe it's a new, better-paying job with a boss who treats you with more respect or one that gives you more of a chance to make a difference. It could be you're searching for the right person to marry or are struggling to drop those extra twenty pounds you feel are holding you back.

I'm going to let you in on a secret: You've already got everything you need to be happy.

You don't need to land a new job or change your career. You don't need to find a mate or lose weight. You don't need to buy a car or move to the country. Being happy requires no change in your personal, work, or financial life. You can find happiness without going to a gym, church, or bank. You don't need anyone else's help to feel fulfilled. There's no need to talk to a plastic surgeon, stockbroker, or career counselor to feel better about yourself and your life.

Right now, you have within you all you need to find fulfillment and lead a happy, satisfying life. It doesn't matter how old you are or how much you earn. It doesn't matter if you're married or single, gay or straight. It doesn't matter where you live or how you look. It doesn't matter if you've just finished a marathon or you've been diagnosed with cancer. Happiness is within your grasp.

That's because the secrets to happiness are all in your head. Usually the phrase "it's all in your head" is intended as a condescending comment: that whatever it is you're feeling isn't real, that it's a figment of your imagination. But I mean it literally. The keys to a fulfilled, joyous life are all in your head because they're attitudes, not actions. They're ways you need to think, not steps you need to take. True happiness comes not from material, or external, factors, but from psychological, or internal, factors. Happiness is a mental, not a physical, state.

> True happiness comes not from material, or external, factors, but from psychological, or internal, factors. Happiness is a mental, not a physical, state.

The good news is this means each and every one one of us has the potential to be happy. The bad news is your happiness is your own responsibility. You're the only one who can make yourself happy. No one and nothing else can do it for you. Not even me or this book.

What makes it even tougher is there are lots of forces out there preaching you're not responsible. Our consumption-based economy and perfection-obsessed mass culture offer countless keys to happiness. Slim down following the latest diet and bulk up using the newest fitness regime or piece of equipment and you'll be happy. If those don't work, have plastic surgery or take steroids. After all, the stars do it and they're happy. You'll feel good about yourself if you read the right books and, better yet, read them as part of the right reading group. You've got to see the hit play or have front-row seats to the hot concert tour to be happy. If your kids go the right preschool, then the right private school, and finally the right Ivy League university, you'll be happy. To feel good, you need to make a great salary . . . but only by doing a job that offers spiritual rewards. Then use that money to buy the smallest MP3 player and the largest flat-screen television, both of which can be controlled by the remote on the dashboard of that car you need to have. If you're single, that car has to be a quirky import that fits your originality . . . as well as everyone else's individuality. If you're married with kids, it needs to be an armored leviathan capable of transporting a junior high soccer team through Baghdad in safety. That will bring you joy. The right shoes, the right haircut, the right scent, will make you happy. And after buying all that, make sure you've invested all the rest in hedge funds so you can retire at fifty to become a social worker in a developing country.

It's not just the media and commerce that are telling up happiness will come from what we do. Clergy preach you've got to come back to the church to find God. Parents tell us we need to go to a certain college. Our friends who are married tell us we too need to get married. Our siblings who start families tell us we have to do the same, or else we'll never learn what really matters. Every day, in hundreds if not thousands of ways, we're told happiness is available out there, if we just buy or do something.

The Fruitless Pursuit of Happiness

Is it any wonder, then, that many of us have, consciously or not, turned our lives into quests for happiness? We may jump from job to job, maybe even spouse to spouse, looking for fulfillment. We might change locations and hairstyles. Perhaps we repeatedly buy the latest electronic toy and the newest diet book. We may obsess about building up our portfolios and biceps. But the quest always ends in failure. "The search for happiness," wrote the author D. H. Lawrence, "always ends in the ghastly sense of the bottomless nothingness into which you will inevitably fall if you strain any further." The philosopher Albert Camus put it in even blunter terms: "You will never be happy if you continue to search for what happiness consists of. You will never live if you are looking for the meaning of life."

> You will never be happy if you continue to search for what happiness consists of. You will never live if you are looking for the meaning of life.
>
> —Albert Camus

Yet we keep on searching, despite, and perhaps because of, our continuing unhappiness. We keep on banging our heads against the wall. We think happiness must be just around the corner, in our next office, at the party on Friday night, with the person we've met online. The historian and playwright Voltaire was right when he wrote, "Men who seek happiness are like drunkards who can never find their house but are sure they have one." And the more we search, the worse it gets. "Those who wander in the world avowedly and purposely in pursuit of happiness, who view every scene of present joy with an eye to what may succeed," wrote the author Frances Burney, "certainly are more liable to disappointment, misfortune and unhappiness, than those who give up their fate to chance and take the goods and evils of fortune as they come, without making happiness their study, or misery their foresight." In other words, the more we devote ourselves to the pursuit of happiness, the more unhappy we get.

A wonderful example of the futility of the pursuit comes from the film *Chariots of Fire*,* based on the true stories of British track athletes competing in the 1924 Summer Olympics. One of its major plot lines involves Harold Abrahams, a Jewish student at Cambridge University. Abrahams, played by Ben Cross, is determined not only to triumph in his race—the 100-meter dash—but to triumph over anti-Semitism and class prejudice in the process. He seems to feel that only by being victorious over external obstacles will he be happy. After winning the race and becoming the fastest man alive, Abrahams explains to a teammate who didn't win a race that despite all Abrahams's external victories, he's still feeling empty: "You, Aubrey, are my most complete man. You're a brave, compassionate, kind, and content man. That's your secret—contentment. I'm forever in pursuit, and I don't even know what it is I'm chasing."

Part of our problem today, one reason we so readily look for happiness through materialism, is that we confuse pleasure with happiness. The former is a sensual feeling, the latter is spiritual. The British broadcaster Malcom Muggeridge once noted, "The pursuit of happiness in any case soon resolved itself into the pursuit of pleasure—something quite different. Pleasure is but a mirage of happiness—a false vision of shade and refreshment seen across parched sand." Pleasure, whether it comes from eating a fine meal or listening to a brilliantly per-

*Written by Colin Welland and directed by Hugh Hudson.

formed symphony, is a physical sensation. Happiness, on the other hand, is a psychological sensation of fulfillment and satisfaction. As the author Franz Kafka wrote, perfect happiness is "to believe in the indestructible element within one." Pleasure, by its very nature, is transitory, while happiness can be permanent.

> Part of our problem today, one reason we so readily look for happiness through materialism, is that we confuse pleasure with happiness. The former is a sensual feeling, the latter is spiritual.

Now, don't get me wrong. I'm all for pleasure. In fact, I suggest you get as much of it as you can. I certainly do. I had some fun earlier in this chapter joking about excessive materialism, but truth be told, I'm as guilty as most. I love dining out at fine restaurants. My wife and I regularly go to performances of the New York Philharmonic Orchestra. We have a beautiful apartment in Manhattan, a weekend house in the country, and a summer house on Martha's Vineyard. In no way am I suggesting you give up the things that bring you pleasure. I haven't and don't intend do. There's nothing wrong with buying a new pair of skis because they tickle your fancy or ordering the lobster if you're in the mood. Life is short, so if you can afford to indulge a bit now and then, go for it. What matters is you realize these indulgences won't bring happiness.

Instead of looking for happiness, you need to start listening for it. Close your eyes and open your ears. The simple truth is, nothing external will make you happy. Harold Abrahams learned that even after winning an Olympic gold medal and triumphing over bigotry and prejudice. Nothing you can see will bring fulfillment to your life. You can lose all the weight you want, find a wonderful life partner, get a fabulous job that pays you an incredible salary, buy a magnificent home and furnish it with everything you've dreamed, and you'll still be unhappy. You can have none of these things and be happy. You can get pleasure from external factors, but happiness is an inside job. It requires listening to your heart and soul. It has nothing to do with the physical facts of your life and everything to do with your attitude toward life. "Does not happiness come from the soul within?" asked the novelist Honoré de Balzac. The poet Nathaniel Cotton agreed, writing: "If solid happiness we prize, / Within our breast this jewel lies, / And they are fools who roam. / The world has nothing to bestow; / From our own selves our joys must flow, / And that dear hut, our home." Putting a lighter, more modern spin on this notion, the novelist Robertson Davies wrote, "Happiness is always a by-product. It is probably a matter of temperament, and for anything I know it may be glandular."

Happiness is always a by-product. It is probably a matter of temperament, and for anything I know it may be glandular.
—Robertson Davies

All Unhappiness Is Bad

I certainly don't mean to make light of unhappiness by quoting Davies or by saying happiness is so readily available to us all. There's real suffering in the world. There's pain and sorrow and misery and guilt and grief. Lots of it. There's an old Jewish folktale of a woman who, distraught over the death of her only son, asks her rabbi to give her a prayer that will bring him back from the dead. The rabbi tells her that to perform the ritual, she needs to bring him back a mustard seed from a house where there's no sorrow. The woman begins searching her town. She goes to every house, from the largest mansion to the smallest shack, searching for a house without sorrow from which to take a mustard seed. But she finds that every person has, in one way or another, experienced pain and unhappiness.

Your realizing happiness is all in your head and adopting a different approach to life isn't like finding a magic mustard seed. It won't add a single day to the life of a child suffering from leukemia or erase the pain of a Holocaust survivor. And it certainly won't bring back the dead. But it can bring joy to your life right here and now. A new attitude may not be able to change the world, but it can change your world. And that's nothing to sneeze at. The world is changed one person at a time.

A new attitude may not be able to change the world, but it can change your world.

Let's face it, if you're like many us, your unhappiness isn't anywhere near as profound as the agony experienced by someone who saw a loved one die or has suffered some other terrible trauma. Some of you may be feeling that kind of pain, but for most of us, feelings of unhappiness stem from a dissatisfaction with the circumstances of our lives. Still, psychological and emotional pain can be as debilitating as physical pain; battered self-esteem can be as incapacitating as a broken leg. As Neil Young sang, "Though my problems are meaningless, that don't make them go away."*

Unhappiness is never good. Whether you're feeling miserable

*From the song "On the Beach."

because of some type of actual physical trauma to you or loved ones, or you're depressed because you feel somehow inadequate, it's essential you free yourself from the grip of unhappiness. The philosopher William James wrote, "The attitude of unhappiness is not only painful, it is mean and ugly. What can be more base and unworthy than the pining, puling, mumping mood, no matter by what outward ills it may have been engendered? What is more injurious to others? What less helpful as a way out of the difficulty? It but fastens and perpetuates the trouble which occasioned it, and increases the total evil of the situation. At all costs, then, we ought to reduce the sway of that mood; we ought to scout it in ourselves and others, and never show it tolerance."

There is a way to make your unhappiness go away, to show it no tolerance. Whether you're unhappy about how your life isn't measuring up to expectations, or you're depressed because you received a frightening medical diagnosis, you can be happy right now. You already have all the tools you need inside your head, and it's never too late to find fulfillment. Gustave Flaubert wrote, "Happiness is like smallpox: If you catch it too soon, it can completely ruin your constitution." I guess I've got a great constitution, because it took me more than seventy years to figure all this out. Well, better late than never.

Confessions of a Serial Problem Solver

My name is Stephen M. Pollan. I'm a life strategist working in New York City. Although I'm an attorney, I began my working life as a real estate entrepreneur on Long Island. I then became president of an American Stock Exchange–listed venture capital firm and next moved into banking. During my time as a Wall Street banker, I suffered a serious illness that caused me to lose my job at age forty-eight and change career directions. (I'll tell you all about it in a subsequent chapter.) After recovering, I launched a private legal practice. That was almost thirty years ago.

From day one of my private practice, I focused on solving the problems of my clients. Early on, most of those problems revolved around credit and real estate issues, so my practice centered on offering home-buying advice and help. Then, many of my clients began exploring business opportunities, so I began to work on solving their entrepreneurial problems. Next, as my nonentrepreneurial clients moved up corporate ladders, I began helping them solve their employment problems. Most recently I've been working with clients who, as they start to reach middle age, want to reinvent their personal and work lives.

Throughout this evolution, I was always in touch with the entire mosaic of problems clients were experiencing, both personal and professional, emotional as well as financial and legal. That's because I take an intimate and holistic approach to my consultations. You see, I believe it's a mistake to see our lives as a set of distinct and separate threads. I feel you need to factor your entire life into decisions and problem solving in order to create unified life strategies. For instance, how much money you have in the bank, your health, your desire to start a family, your spouse's desire for a garden, and your status at work should all factor into your home-buying decisions. Because I'm just as likely to discuss birthing as investing with a client, I've become deeply involved in people's lives.

As my life strategy practice evolved, I sometimes wondered what problematic area of life I'd be dealing with next. I saw the lives of my clients as journeys down life paths that had, along with them, an undetermined number of hurdles. I felt my job was to help my clients come up with tactics to overcome the specific obstacle they were facing at that moment, and then, when they confronted another obstacle, I'd help them develop ways to scale that as well.

It was only after doing this for nearly thirty years, and having my seventy-fifth birthday in sight, that I realized I'd been helping them with tactics when I should have been helping them develop a strategy; I was treating my clients' symptoms rather than their disease.

Treating the Disease Rather Than the Symptoms

Over the years, my clients have been African American, Asian, and Caucasian. I've worked with singles as well as couples, gays as well as straights. Hindus, Jews, Muslims, Christians, pagans, and atheists have all sat across the desk from me. But because of the nature of what I do and where I do it, my clients do generally fit a particular profile: they're almost all upper middle class or affluent, they're primarily city dwellers, and nearly all are professionals or managers.

As I've helped them overcome the problems they've faced, I've also noticed that no matter how their incomes soared and their assets grew, regardless of how many homes they bought, they always expressed some degree of unhappiness. No matter how many battles we won with the tactics I'd given them, they weren't winning the war. It didn't matter if their marriages were wonderful and they had a passel of high-achieving children. They could be lithe triathletes who'd look at home on the cover of *Glamour* or *Men's Health*. Throughout this book I'll be telling their specific stories, and the stories of other people I've met, but for now let me just note that regardless of their specific external successes and achievements, most of the people I know find reasons to be unhappy with their lives.

I don't think these people are, in this matter, any different from the general population. When the great poet Philip Larkin was asked to comment on his being named poet laureate, he said, "I think writing about unhappiness is probably the source of my popularity, if I have any—after all, most people are unhappy, don't you think?" The aphorist Mason Cooley joked, "Unhappiness is too common to call for special measures."

What makes the people I know different is that they represent a very affluent, successful group. That just makes the dichotomy between their external success and internal unhappiness all the more striking. Like most of us, they have what I like to call a "worry box" inside their heads: a place to store fears, doubts, worries, qualms, uncertainties, and concerns. Every time we do something to empty that worry box of whatever is troubling us, we find some way to fill it up again.

> Every time we do something to empty that worry box of whatever is troubling us, we find some way to fill it up again.

Now, I'm very good at what I do. When my clients face obstacles or problems, I'm almost always able to help them overcome and flourish. But despite all my efforts at helping prosperous clients surmount hurdle after hurdle, I found that they remained unfulfilled and dissatisfied with their lives; they continued to find ways to fill their worry boxes. And that was frustrating. I don't know whether it's ego driven, guilt induced, or due to an unquenchable need to be loved, but I felt and continue to feel the need to help my clients not just succeed, but be as happy in their lives as possible. I wanted to start treating the underlying disease of unhappiness, not just the visible symptoms. I wanted to offer them a life strategy that would win them happiness.

I'm not a psychotherapist. Nor am I a philosopher or a theologian. I don't claim to have their insights or therapeutic skills.

But my longtime collaborator, Mark Levine, and I have become very good at figuring out ways for people to solve their problems. We decided to address the search for happiness in the same way we'd addressed all the goals we'd written about over the past twenty years. That meant developing a practical approach to being happy. I think we've done that by outlining a set of attitudes you need to adopt to find fulfillment in the life you have.

You're Not in Kansas Anymore

Before I get into just what those attitudes are, let me explain why you may find they sound familiar. It's because on some level you already know this stuff. Mark and I haven't discovered a set of previously unknown secrets to life. What we've done is look at the attitudes we believe may be making you unhappy and then look for new attitudes you can adopt that will help make you happy. In the process, we realized these new helpful attitudes are already among the vast store of accumulated wisdom to which we've all been exposed through school, religious instruction, and popular culture. They're ideas we've learned but somehow set aside or forgot. Perhaps it's because, as the educator Thomas Henry Huxley noted, "pain and sorrow knock at our doors more loudly than pleasure and happiness; and the prints of their heavy footsteps are less easily effaced." I think we've overlooked simple truths because we feel our unhappiness is so profound, it could be overcome only through dramatic gestures and sophisticated philosophies. In our increasingly complex world, it's counterintuitive that the secrets to happiness are simple and existent. But they are. The secrets to happiness are all in your head, not just because they're attitudes, but because they're truths we learned at some point in our lives but have either overlooked or forgotten.

The secrets to happiness are all in your head, not just because they're attitudes, but because they're truths we learned at some point in our lives but have either overlooked or forgotten.

In writing this book, I feel a bit like the Wizard in the movie version of *The Wizard of Oz*.* If you remember, at the end of the film, Dorothy, the Scarecrow, the Cowardly Lion, and the Tin Man finally get to present their requests to the Wizard of Oz. Dorothy, played by Judy Garland, wanted to learn how to get back to Kansas. The Scarecrow, played by Ray Bolger, wanted a brain. The Lion, played by Bert Lahr, wanted courage. And the Tin Man, played by Jack Haley, wanted a heart. When he hears of their requests, the Wizard, played by Frank Morgan, tells the Cowardly Lion he doesn't need courage since he already has it; the Wizard just gives the Lion a medal to wear. The Wizard tells the Scarecrow that he doesn't need a brain because he's already smart; instead, the Wizard gives the Scarecrow a diploma. Then the Wizard tells the Tin Man that he obviously already has a heart but that what he needs instead is a clock to put inside his chest to tick away regularly. In effect, the Wizard is saying to all three that what they lack is the external acknowledgment of a trait they already possess. And that they need this external acknowledgment not for others, but for themselves. They need someone else to tell them they already have what they need. Finally, the Glinda the Good Witch tells Dorothy she already has the way to get home: Just click the heels of the ruby slippers on her feet three times while saying, "There's no place like home," and she'll return to Kansas. Like

---

*The film, directed by Victor Fleming and written by Noel Langley, Florence Ryerson, and Edgar Allan Woolf, was based on the books by L. Frank Baum.

her three friends, Dorothy already had what she sought; she had the tools, she just didn't know how to use them.

That's my message to you as well. Like the Cowardly Lion, you already have the courage to do what you must to be fulfilled. Like the Scarecrow, you already have the wisdom to choose the paths that will make you satisfied. Like the Tin Man, you already have the heart and faith to follow your bliss. And like Dorothy, you have the tools to be happy today. You don't have to put on ruby slippers, however; you just need to change some of your attitudes.

Since happiness is based on internal factors, you need to examine your attitudes toward yourself and your role in the world if you want to find fulfillment. I can't sit down with each one of you to explore your own attitudes and how you see yourself in relation to the universe, as I would if you were in my office for a consultation. The most I can do in the format of a book is offer some generalizations that I've found fit the vast majority of my clients, friends, family, and acquaintances and, I believe, will fit the vast majority of readers. Together, Mark and I have gone back over my practice for the past three decades and my life for the past seven decades. We've discovered there are eight attitudes that we believe are leading people to keep their worry boxes filled. In effect, they're the ways you're thinking yourself into unhappiness. By reaching inside your head and turning those attitudes around, you can start thinking your way to happiness.

We Measure Ourselves Against Others

I'm always amazed at how people, no matter how successful, are able to find some part of their lives in which they don't measure up. We compare ourselves to others in millions of different ways. What's our salary as compared with those of our co-workers? How does our house compare with our sibling's? What cars do we and our neighbors drive? Are we in better shape than our friend? Are our children going to more prestigious colleges than our nephews and nieces?

As I'll explain in chapter 2, this kind of comparing will make you miserable. You're entering not just one but hundreds of races you can never win. And in the process you're doing things not for yourself, but for others. The truth is that you're just where you're supposed to be.

We're Pessimistic About the Future

I've seen people let dramatic events or milestones in their lives shift their outlook from hopeful to hopeless about their future. Millions of us spend thousands of dollars and hundreds of hours fighting the passage of time. Like King Knute trying to hold back the tide, we try to hold back the hands of the clock, thinking that every minute that passes is another minute closer to death.

Viewing the passage of time as a negative factor guarantees unhappiness. After all, time will pass and there's nothing you can do to stop it. Instead of fighting, embrace time. In chapter 3, I'll show how it leads to wisdom, eases pain, lessens anger, and adds perspective. Every year that passes is a cause to celebrate, because things get better.

We Are Our Own Worst Enemies

I've seen people say things about themselves they'd never let anyone else get away with. And I'm sure their thoughts were worse than their statements. I'm not talking about constructive self-criticism; I'm talking about self-denigration that does nothing but lower self-esteem. Few of us seem willing to accept compliments or acknowledge our own victories. In order to be happy, we need to be able to see ourselves realistically—the good as well as the bad.

Chapter 4 will encourage you to cultivate an attitude of humility and to get out from between your ears to start seeing yourself realistically. Believe it or not, surrender will increase your self-esteem and let you finally own your success.

We Think Needing and Asking for Help Is a Sign of Weakness

We've been taught it's better to accomplish things on our own, that the greatest success is being self-made. As little children we're praised for it—"You did that all by yourself"—as students we're schooled in it, and as adults we idolize it. Underlying this religion of individualism is the fear that no one would help us out anyway. But by not asking for help, we fail to take advantage of all the tools at our disposal to be happy.

Rugged individualism and the lack of helpfulness in the world are two other myths that lock unhappiness in place. In chapter 5, I'll describe how realizing you don't have to go it alone is vital to being happy.

We Wait for the Best Time or the Right Time

I've found the almost universal reaction to confronting decisions or facing new situations is to delay or procrastinate. Sometimes it's in a search for the right or best time. Other times it's because we're afraid of failing. Whatever the reason, hesitation almost always leads to unhappiness. By delaying an action, we only delay happiness and freeze fear in place.

In chapter 6, I'll explain that waiting for the right or best time means waiting forever, since you can't know that moment until it has passed. I'll also describe how procrastination increases rather than reduces fears. The answer is to realize there's no time like now, so take the action.

We Think We Can Have Everything

We have been raised to believe all barriers to individual advancement have been torn down and that we have the freedom to achieve whatever we set out to and experience whatever we choose. But while our freedoms may be limitless, our finances and time are limited, and getting more so every day. That leads to incredible frustration and unhappiness. By trying to have everything, and failing, we feel as though we have nothing.

The answer is that happiness comes from having a well-rounded life. For most of us, a life in which you make compromises and pick your spots will provide more fulfillment than one in which you dedicate yourself single-mindedly to the pursuit of being the best in one area. It's time to realize, as I'll note in chapter 7, that you don't have to be the best—doing your best is enough.

We Spend Time Reliving and Regretting the Past

It's incredible how many of us spend time looking backward. Some are angry with others because of what they did to us or didn't do for us. Some regret things they did or things they failed to do. While it's okay, even helpful, to briefly look back at good times, it's harmful to dwell on past injuries or failings. Since we can't change what has already happened, focusing on the past locks us into permanent victimhood and unhappiness.

To be happy today, you need to stop living in the past, give up your victimhood, and embrace an image of yourself as an empowered person. In chapter 8, I describe how to do that by forgiving others and yourself and realizing the past is past.

We Spend Too Much Time Dreaming of the Future

When we're not wasting time by looking backward in anger, we're sapping our energies by looking forward in hope. By spending our lives planning and hoping and dreaming, we lose sight of what our life is today. We give up an opportunity for happiness today by focusing on tomorrow.

I think part of the problem is that we view the present solely as the blink of an eye, a moment that lies between the past and the future. If instead we see the present as the life we're leading and try to live "in the now," we'll find happiness. Today is the experience of living and being happy, not a time for remembering or hoping. As I explain in chapter 9, by taking responsibility for our own joy, we can stop deferring fulfillment to a nonexistent tomorrow and be happy today. We need to realize tomorrow is too late.

How to Use This Book

Each of the subsequent chapters in this book is a discussion of one of these changes of attitude we believe you need to make to be happy today. The order in which they're presented is based solely on making the narrative flow as naturally as possible. If you find it easiest to work on the attitude adjustments in a different order, that's fine. Do whatever works best for you. Similarly, the exercises we describe in each chapter are intended as suggestions and tips, not prescriptions. If you were sitting across the desk from me in my office, we could work together to develop custom exercises. The ones offered here are of necessity developed for the widest audience possible. If you come up with exercises of your own that feel more natural to you or you think will work better, that's fine.

Many of the exercises outlined involve writing lists or thoughts into what Mark and I call a journal. I'm a big believer in writing things down and then keeping those notes. Memorializing your thoughts, ideas, conclusions, and decisions in this manner not only helps you organize the material, but gives you a chance to go back to it later when you feel the need for review or refreshment. The form of these notes is entirely up to you. In this book, we call it a journal and describe it as a notebook, but it could just as easily be a set of index cards or a file on your PDA. What matters is that you're comfortable with the form and are able to preserve it.

At the end of each chapter is a box of what I consider to be the most important points to remember. If you ever need a quick refresher course and don't have the time to reread an entire chapter, you can simply refer to the concluding box.

Quite a few readers of our past books have told me they read them all the way through without doing any of the exercises, then return to the exercises later after absorbing the ideas. To make that process easier, we've included an appendix that brings together all the exercises in one place.

A Few Words About God

In the pages that follow, we mention God quite a bit, far more than we have in any of our previous books. I think I owe you a short explanation. I believe in God. That belief took root in my head, heart, and soul when I realized I wasn't God. I learned I wasn't all-powerful and all-knowing. I accepted that there was a power greater than me. I choose to call that power God, but you can call it whatever you like. You can call it Allah or Jehovah. You can perceive it as being personified by Jesus or Vishnu. You can think of it as a mystical energy or the sum total of all the natural laws of the universe. You can see it as a universal force we can all eventually become a part of, or one we already have within us, or as a great watchmaker who put all the mechanisms in place and just sits and observes. What matters, and what I think is essential in being happy today, is realizing you're not the center of the universe. I mean, how are you going to find the time to be happy if you're busy keeping all the planets in alignment?

I believe in God. That belief took root in my head, heart, and soul when I realized I wasn't God.

I realize we might be going out on a bit of a limb by writing about God. Today it seems everyone is studying public writings and statements with an eye toward somehow characterizing the author, or in this case authors. There are people who, for whatever reason, are actively looking to divide the world into two camps: us and them. We're not going to play that game. When I was a banker and venture capitalist, I used to joke that I saw everyone as being the same color: green. I believe that to God there's just us; there is no them.

Mark and I have done everything we can think of to help you find fulfillment through the pages of this book. But the rest is up to you. Remember, you are responsible for your own happiness. The philosopher Walter Benjamin wrote, "Each morning the day lies like a fresh shirt on our bed; this incomparably fine, incomparably tightly woven tissue of pure prediction fits us perfectly. The happiness of the next twenty-four hours depends on our ability, on waking, to pick it up." Turn the page and be happy.

It's All in Your Head

- Happiness doesn't come from actions, it comes from attitudes. The secrets to happiness are all in your head.
- We confuse pleasure with happiness. The former is sensual and temporary, the latter is spiritual and permanent.
- You have the tools to be happy today. All it takes is changing your attitudes toward yourself and your place in the world.
- The secrets are also already in your head, since they're eternal truths we've learned and either ignored or forgotten.
- Instead of thinking ourselves to unhappiness by living out harmful attitudes, we can think ourselves to happiness by adopting healthy attitudes.
- Don't compare yourself to others. You're just where you're supposed to be.
- Don't be pessimistic about the future. Things get better.
- Stop being your own worst enemy: Own your success.
- Asking for help isn't a sign of weakness: You don't have to go it alone.
- Don't wait for the best or right time: There's no time like now, so take the action.
- You don't need the best: Your best is enough.
- Stop looking backward in anger and regret: The past is past.
- Stop living in the future: Tomorrow is too late.

(2)

YOU'RE JUST WHERE YOU'RE SUPPOSED TO BE

O Lord, won't you buy me a Mercedes-Benz?
My friends all drive Porsches, I must make
amends.

—*Janis Joplin*

D o you sometimes find yourself envying other people? There's no reason. You are incomparable. Your path through life is unique. Your lifelong journey follows a singular trajectory and matchless pattern. You're just where you're supposed to be.

Sure, there are people, even entire groups, who are traveling on paths similar to yours. Maybe you all share the same faith or ethnic background. Perhaps you all grew up in similar circumstances or locations. It's even possible you and they have similar families, went to the same college, or have pursued the same career. But whatever the external parallels, you're all as different internally as your individual DNA-based genetic signatures. The more science learns about how our brains work, the more we realize just how infinitely complex and unique we are.

The more science learns about how our brains work, the more
we realize just how infinitely complex and unique we are.

In his novel *A Tale of Two Cities*, Charles Dickens created
two characters who, while almost identical physically, have dramatically different approaches to life: Charles Darnay is idealis-
tic and altruistic, while his "twin," Sydney Carton, is reckless
and lazy. It's easy for us all to accept that similarities in appearance don't make for similar characters, but that's true for nearly
every other factor. Mikal Gilmore is a well-respected journalist
and critic who has covered music and culture for many national
publications, including *LA Weekly* and the *Los Angeles Herald
Examiner*. His profiles of the famous have appeared in the
pages of *Rolling Stone* for more than twenty years. His first
book won the Los Angeles Times Book Prize and the National
Book Critics Circle Award. It's called *Shot in the Heart,* and it's
about his older brother, the infamous murderer Gary Gilmore.°
    It takes countless ingredients to make a human being. Your
relations to your parents and siblings and friends and lovers,
your physical health and abilities, your upbringing and education, your experiences at work and at play, the books you read
and the movies you see, the teams you follow and the music you
listen to, the places you live and visit, the singular tragedies and
triumphs of your life, and yes, your distinctive genetic material
and your unique relationship to God all play roles in making
you who you are. There's simply no reason to assume your life
should follow the same schedule or direction as anyone else's,
even if they look just like you or grew up in the same house. Yet
many, if not most, of us seem to fall into what I call "the comparison trap."

°Anchor, 1995.

The Comparison Trap

We compare ourselves to others in dozens of ways, from the sublime to the ridiculous.

You worry you're not earning more than $100,000 like your friends. You're upset you haven't made VP as quickly as your peers. You're depressed you're in an industry or profession that isn't "hot." Your investment and retirement funds aren't as big as those you read about in profiles in *Money*. And your holdings are pedestrian—no hedge funds or Google stock.

Maybe your home doesn't have room for a master bathroom suite, or it's not in an area profiled in the real estate section of the Sunday paper. Perhaps your friends have all bought vacation or weekend homes on the shore, while you're still renting a bungalow at the lake. It could be your brother and his wife just put in an in-ground pool or a Viking range and a Sub-Zero refrigerator, while you're still making do with the community pool and the old Kenmore.

You're down because while you're driving a five-year-old minivan, every other car in the mall parking lot is now a brand-new Lexus SUV. Worse yet, unlike the neighbor's new Sienna, your Chevy Astra doesn't have a backseat DVD player for the kids, automatic doors, or a satellite radio receiver.

Your friends in the city have tickets to the latest hit play or the hot show at the downtown gallery, while you're in the suburbs waiting for the DVDs of last year's Oscar-nominated films to arrive from Netflix.

Your children are still going to the local public school rather than the private academy preferred by some of your neighbors. Your dog is a lovable but undisciplined mutt rather than a Labradoodle trained to separate the recycling.

Okay, I've engaged in some hyperbole for easy laughs, but I

know firsthand it's a serious problem and that the sense of being "behind," being a "loser," can be painful.

When I was a little boy, a local newspaper ran a daily feature
on "successful men." My father would come home from his job
selling milk and eggs and make sure to clip that column so it
was sitting on my pillow each night. Although I know it wasn't
his intent, the message I received was, "Your mother and I
won't love you unless you're as successful as these men." My
youthful interest was in radio, but when I was offered the
chance to get into a special program that would grant me a law
degree rather than just a bachelor's degree, my parents made
clear which path they thought a "successful" young man would
pursue.

Later on, when I was married and just starting out, I compared myself to my father-in-law. He was an entirely self-made
man who became very successful financially. He helped my
wife and me out when we bought our first home. Whenever he
would come over to visit, he'd stroll around our house as if he
were the owner. Don't get me wrong: I respected and learned a
great deal from my father-in-law. But while he probably didn't
mean it, he subtly (and sometimes not so subtly) let me know I
wasn't measuring up to his achievements.

My own comparison trap contributed to my becoming a
workaholic and, in retrospect, not being there for my wife and
children. When I was young I was too busy "climbing Mount
Olympus" to be present emotionally for my family.

It's not just my personal experience that has led me to explore
the comparison trap. I've seen it in my clients, family, and
friends as well.

I've listened to Jack Epstein,* thirty-nine, tell me of the pain

*The names of people cited as examples throughout this book have been changed to pro-
tect their privacy.

he feels about not being able to buy his youngest son a new set of goalie pads for his "Squirt" hockey season. Jack, a solidly built and usually gregarious sort, is between jobs, and the family is relying on his wife's salary. Most of the other kids come from well-off families and start each season with new equipment. Jack knows it isn't nearly as terrible as, say, not being able to buy his son a new winter coat, and that his son's old pads are still usable, but try explaining that to a ten-year-old.

Sinead Campbell, forty-six, has told me how demoralized she feels each year at her salary review. A striking woman with short black hair, Sinead is a midlevel editor at a daily newspaper. She has seen people who started in the business when she did move on to its top levels and earn over $150,000. She's still plugging away in the trenches and has yet to earn half that. Worse still, people younger and less experienced are starting to be promoted over her. She knows she should be glad she has a job in this tenuous employment market, but it hurts nevertheless.

I've heard Karen Dishman, fifty-one, speak of the desperation she and her husband, Jimmy, fifty-three, feel about not yet being able to buy a summer house on Martha's Vineyard or Nantucket. Karen, a slight, serious young woman, is an attorney, and Jimmy, a plain-looking fellow with curly black hair and a bushy salt-and-pepper beard, is a college professor. All the other law partners, and most of the clients with whom Karen deals, have summer homes "on the islands." Karen and Jimmy, affluent by any realistic measure, could easily buy a vacation home in a less trendy area. But that won't cut it in their social circle.

I've been moved while listening to Bobby Michaels, thirty-one, talk about the shame he feels at being so far behind his peers. Bobby, a tall, olive-skinned young man with a crew cut, has just graduated college. When he first dropped out of college back when he was nineteen, he planned on becoming a painter.

Then he flirted with an acting career. All the while, he held menial service industry jobs and ignored his growing drinking problem. He bottomed out, sobered up, and started over. Although his recovery is an inspiration to his family and friends, he's embarrassed at being a thirty-one-year-old who's living like a twenty-one-year-old, in a shared apartment on a starting teacher's salary, while all his friends are not just married and established, but are buying homes and starting families.

I know it's much easier to feel sympathy for someone like Bobby than for the Dishmans. And someone who's really struggling might have a hard time feeling for Jack or Sinead. But before you make judgments about the validity of others' pain, realize it doesn't hurt them any less than Bobby's pain hurts him. The issue isn't whether or not someone has a right to be unhappy about themselves or their situation. The issue is that no one should be comparing themselves to others.

The issue isn't whether or not someone has a right to be unhappy about themselves or their situation. The issue is that no one should be comparing themselves to others.

Grant the Dishmans their pain and you grant yourself the pain you might feel over equally trivial matters. It really doesn't matter whether you perceive yourself coming up short in a vital or frivolous aspect of life. What matters is that despite your uniqueness, you compare yourself to others, judge yourself a failure, lower your self-esteem, and feel unhappy.*

---

*Although I don't come across it as often, there's another type of comparison trap: believing others don't measure up to you. Maybe it's expressed in a professional father thinking the working-class family into which his daughter is marrying isn't "good enough." Or it could be one woman thinking a friend doesn't eat as well as she should. It's initially very hard to feel sympathetic for people who have this kind of attitude. But this sense of superiority is actually indicative of even *lower* self-esteem. The only way an elitist can make him- or herself feel good is at the expense of others.

I think one of the most poignant examples of this downward spiral of comparing comes from Francis Ford Coppola's films *The Godfather* and *The Godfather: Part II.*° Alfredo, played by John Cazale, is the oldest son of Vito Corleone, played by Marlon Brando. Perhaps as the result of contracting a high fever when he was an infant, Fredo is a bit slow. His younger brothers, Santino ("Sonny"), played by James Caan, and Michael, played by Al Pacino, each in turn take over the running of the crime family. Fredo is first relegated to being his father's driver and then given unimportant jobs in Las Vegas and Havana. Despite having a warmth and generosity of spirit neither of his brothers possesses, Fredo is always comparing himself to his younger brothers. When Michael says, "I'll always take care of you," Fredo snaps, "You'll take care of me! I'm the older brother!" Fredo's sense of not measuring up to his brothers eventually leads him to turn on Michael, which subsequently leads to his own destruction.

Why Do We Do This to Ourselves?

You compare yourself to others for the same reason I did: You were taught the behavior.

We aren't born with the tendency to measure ourselves against others and then feel bad about the result. Nature doesn't work that way. Newborns aren't lying around the hospital nursery checking out who's thinner or who has the most hair. And toddlers who play together aren't trying to figure out whose blocks are imported from Germany and whose are hand-me-downs. But in just a few years, little children start to slowly but surely fall into the comparison trap.

°Both films were directed by Coppola and written by Coppola and Mario Puzo, author of the novel on which they were based.

Newborns aren't lÿing around the hospital nursery checking out who's thinner or who has the most hair. And toddlers who play together aren't trying to figure out whose blocks are imported from Germany and whose are hand-me-downs.

Partly that's due to the way they're raised. All parents make mistakes. As the father of four, I can attest to that. In retrospect, I see how my own parents contributed to my comparison trap. It's easy to see where it came from. My parents were working-class people who desperately wanted their children to climb into the middle class. As the oldest, I was the one who "broke the trail." From the clippings on my pillow to the encouragement of a legal career, I was "groomed" to measure my success against my parents' standards. Whether this was due to my father feeling like a failure, to my mother feeling that as a woman she didn't have a chance to live up to her potential, or to some other deep psychological motivation doesn't really matter. What matters is that I was taught to measure myself against external standards.

My upbringing in a time of less "enlightened" child rearing might seem like an extreme example. But baby boomers were raised with just as many expectations, probably more. Boomers were going to be the generation that "saved" the world. And today, the children of boomers are being taught to compare themselves as well. Sometimes it seems children have busier daily schedules than their parents. What parent hasn't reflexively asked his or her child, "How did your friends do on the test?" or some similar question that forces comparison? Baby boomers are snaring their children in the comparison trap just as they were snared and my generation was snared.

Don't get me wrong. I'm not trying to blame all this on parents. That's both unfair and an oversimplification. Parents do this to their kids—have always done this to their kids—not because the act of reproduction automatically creates a critic, but because we live in a society that encourages, maybe even demands, measurement and comparison.

Whatever its faults, America is as close to a meritocracy as any nation in the history of the world. The clichés and bromides are true: Anyone can succeed in America. At our best, we don't judge someone by his parents or her color, his religion or her ethnicity. Ours isn't a class-based or tribal-oriented society.

But on the flip side, we too often judge based on external and material factors. In order to determine who has merit, we look for ways to compare and see who comes out on top.

Since we're a strongly individualistic and capitalist society, we instinctively look to economic and material factors as the primary yardsticks. We judge by how well someone does on her exams in school, by how many widgets he produces or hours he bills at work, how much money she earns for the company or for herself. Then there are times we judge by the clothes people wear, the cars they drive, the homes in which they live. From poor young men in the inner city who measure one another by the sneakers they wear to corporate execs who measure one another by the type of boat they dock at the yacht club, we've all been encouraged to use material quantitative factors for self-measurement.

I guess what I'm saying is that parents are the unwitting means by which the comparison trap is passed from American society at large to individuals. They're the carriers of the disease, not its cause.

Comparing Is a Deadly Habit

It may sound harsh to say comparing yourself to others is a disease, but I really believe it's like a slow-growing cancer on your soul. It may not kill your spirit overnight, but little by little, year by year, it destroys your chances for happiness. The medieval monk and author Baltasar Gracián wrote, "The envious person dies not once, but as often as his rival lives in applause."

> The envious person dies not once, but as often as his rival lives in applause.
>
> —Baltasar Gracián

Material possessions aren't inherently bad. A Mercedes 300 isn't evil. It's the endless and constant pursuit of material possessions, and the belief that those possessions have the power to make you happy, that is problematic. You see, the more you have, the more you end up wanting. The pursuit of material possessions is like an addiction. Once you start, you can't stop.

There's a wonderful Hindu story about an earnest young seeker who goes to a wise man and asks for advice on how he can achieve spiritual enlightenment. The wise man tells the young seeker to renounce material possessions. The young seeker eagerly sells all he owns, except for a loincloth, and begins wandering the countryside. After only a few days of wandering, the young seeker decides to sit by a stream and wash his loincloth. He hangs the loincloth in a tree branch to dry and takes a nap. When the young seeker awakes, he finds that birds have pecked holes in his loincloth. He decides to go to a nearby village and beg for another loincloth. In the village, a kindly woman gives the young seeker a new loincloth but says, "You don't need just a loincloth, you also need a cat to protect your loincloth from the birds." The young seeker, seeing the logic in her suggestion, begs for a cat and later that day is given one. The next day, while continuing his travels, he realizes he needs milk for his cat. He goes to another village to beg for milk. A friendly man gives him some milk but suggests he needs to get a cow so he'll always have milk for his cat. The young seeker begs for a cow and later that day is given one. On the road, now with his cat and his cow, the young seeker soon realizes he needs hay to feed the cow. He goes to yet another village, where's he's told it's better to beg for a farm so he'll always have hay for his cow. He's given a farm but realizes he needs help to run it. He hires laborers. Soon he marries and has children. Next he becomes a businessman, owning multiple farms. Years go by, and the wise man, wondering what became of the earnest young seeker, sets out on the road to find him. After a few days of wandering, he comes to a magnificent hilltop mansion where he decides to beg for a meal. The wise man knocks on the door. The formerly young seeker opens the door, sees the wise man, and falls to the ground in tears, stammering, "It all began with a loincloth."

It begins with just a loincloth for all of us. Unfortunately, there is always more we think we need. The more you possess, the more you need to possess. Owning something leads you to own other things to store and clean and improve the first thing you possess. Buy a telephone and you need an answering machine, and extension cords, and a caller ID system, and surge protectors, and soon a new telephone. First-time home buyers are always amazed at the sheer number of things they need to buy now that they have a house. There are hoses and ladders and drills and lawn mowers and rakes and snow shovels. Suddenly those former apartment dwellers realize why Home Depot is so popular. Of course, that's nothing compared with what first-time parents experience. Traveling with an infant or toddler these days is more complex and requires more logistical planning than the invasion of Normandy in World War II.

The problem is that you can never win this race. As Baltasar Gracián wrote, "There is no one who cannot better someone else at something, and there will always be someone who can conquer even him." For example, there will also always be someone wealthier than you, no matter how much money you have. Even if you become the next George Soros, there will always be a new Bill Gates.

And it's not just material quantity that overwhelms us; it's the quality or size or style of possessions. State-of-the-art technologies now seem to become obsolete even before they reach the market. Anything you can buy at a chain store, rather than an electronics boutique, is "retro." Styles change faster than the flavor of the month. Chic wardrobes now require midseason corrections. And fashion now extends beyond clothing, autos, and electronics into biology. People treat pregnancy and stomach stapling as fashion trends and areas for competition.

Entering the style race is just as self-defeating as joining the battle for more. There will always be larger homes than yours, more luxurious or faster cars than yours. Buy an H2 and you'll see someone else has bought a full-size Hummer. There will always be someone who has climbed the business ladder faster than you. Once you get into the hot restaurant, another eatery will soon become the "in" place. The philosopher Arthur Schopenhauer said, "Wealth is like sea-water; the more we drink the thirstier we become." The same is true for every other material or external factor by which you compare yourself to others.

> Wealth is like sea-water; the more we drink the thirstier we become.
>
> —Arthur Schopenhauer

In my practice, I work with some incredibly wealthy people, individuals who wouldn't be able to spend all their money in two lifetimes, let alone one, yet they still hunger for more.

One particular man, Jerry Edwards, fifty-nine, is a very successful real estate entrepreneur, a millionaire many times over; he owns multiple homes around the world and has a chauffeur to drive him, a nanny to watch his children, a live-in maid and cook to help his wife run the houses, and every material luxury one could ever want, yet he obsessively seeks out more wealth. Jerry looks like a heavier version of the actor William Hurt. After a couple of years, Jerry and I got close enough for me to finally ask him about his pursuit of wealth. "You know you don't need more money, Jerry," I said, "so what's driving you?"

"I don't need it," he concurred, "but it's a way to keep score. The more I get, the closer I come to winning."

The problem, of course, is there's no way Jerry, or you, or any of us can win this kind of game. We are all mortal. Because life ends, so must the quest for material things. And since there's always more, you can never get it all. You are destined to run out of time. No matter how long you live, if you look to material possessions for your happiness, you are doomed to die unhappy. Worse still, you are doomed to live unhappy. It's like running a lifelong race in which the finish line is constantly ten yards ahead of you. All you do your entire life is run the race. You can never win the race, and you can't stop running. You spend your whole life pursuing something you can never achieve and not enjoying what you do have.

Those material possessions may provide you with pleasures. And there's nothing wrong with that. Actually, I hope they do provide you with pleasure. There's nothing wrong with wanting nice things or enjoying a neat new convenience. Believe me, I can be as hedonistic as the next person. I have lovely, well-furnished homes and a nice wardrobe, and I've got a serious weakness for halvah. All these things, and others, give me a great deal of pleasure. As long as you're not living beyond your means, buying some pleasure isn't wrong. The problem is that no matter how much pleasure you or I derive from them, they never make us happy. Pleasure is sensual. Happiness is spiritual. Look to material possessions for happiness and you'll be running a race you can never win.

It's sort of like the movie *Groundhog Day*.° In it, Bill Murray plays Phil Connors, an arrogant, self-centered, semi-celebrity weatherman who has been sent to cover the emergence of, in his words, "a weather-forecasting rat" for four straight years. After a day of frustration and cynicism, he awakens to find he has to repeat the same day. Eventually he realizes he is doomed to repeat this same day for all eternity. It doesn't matter what he does, Phil wakes every morning to live the same day over and over again.

Don't think there's some magical level of material or external achievement that, having been reached, will allow you to forgo further material pursuits. Or that there's a degree of pleasure you'll reach that will make you happy. That's just like the smoker who says, "I'll just finish this last pack and then I'll quit," or the alcoholic who says, "I'll give up drinking once I get out of this lousy job." The Japanese poet Yoshida Kenkō wrote, "If you imagine that once you have accomplished your ambitions you will have time to turn to the Way, you will discover that your ambitions never come to an end."

Look Inward Rather Than Outward

I believe the secret to climbing out of this trap and realizing you're just where you're supposed to be is to compare yourself to yourself. Pursue those things that give you pleasure, not things that others pursue or things you think should make you

°Directed by Harold Ramis and written by Ramis and Danny Rubin.

happy. Base decisions on your life, the life you want to lead, not someone else's life or the life others think you should lead.

Many thinkers over the years have eloquently made the case that the key to spiritual enlightenment is the abandonment of materialism. Every major religion seems to have an ascetic branch that preaches and practices an extremely austere life-style. The idea is that by renouncing possessions, you actually also renounce self-will and open yourself to God's will. Francis of Assisi explained that living without property kept him and his followers from ever becoming upset by anything anyone else did.

Base decisions on your life, the life you want to lead, not someone else's life or the life others think you should lead.

There's a wonderful story about the Greek philosopher Diogenes that makes a similar point: The abandonment of materialism offers freedom. Diogenes is sitting on the side of the road eating his simple meal of porridge. A court philosopher sees him and comes over to chat. "You know, Diogenes, if you learned to play up to the king like the rest of us, you wouldn't have to live on porridge." Diogenes doesn't even glance up from his bowl; he just says, "If you learned to live on porridge, you wouldn't have to play up to the king."

There's something to be said for asceticism. Its simplicity and purity appeal to some people on a very fundamental level. In addition, making a shift from twenty-first-century American materialism to asceticism is dramatic. It's a grand gesture, like giving up smoking cold turkey or quitting a job after a slight. And those kinds of bold actions seem heroic and noble. I think that's what accounts for the popularity of recent ascetic trends like extreme frugality and voluntary simplicity.

If the spirit moves you to abandon materialism and enter a

monastery, God bless you. And if you're driven to start growing your own vegetables and simplifying your life, go for it. But do it because you truly want to, not because your favorite actor has become a Buddhist monk or you read an article in *The Wall Street Journal* on the trend toward upscale organic subsistence farmers. Comparing yourself to others by measuring your asceticism or frugality is just as destructive as comparing how much money you earn.

To me, it's the comparing, not the materialism, that's the real problem. I believe one of the keys to happiness is being true to yourself. That means realizing you're just where you're supposed to be. François, Duc de La Rochefoucauld, the writer and moralist, wrote, "Happiness does not consist in things themselves but in the relish we have of them; and a man has attained it when he enjoys what he loves and desires himself, and not what other people think lovely and desirable."

One of my favorite stories is of a famous Polish rabbi named Hafez Hayyim. It's said a very learned man came a great distance to visit and speak with Rabbi Hayyim. On entering the rabbi's home, the traveler is surprised that the small house, while filled with books, has only a table and bench as furniture. The traveler feels compelled to ask, "Rabbi, where's your furniture?" The rabbi responds with a question of his own: "Where's your furniture?" The visitor, taken aback, responds, "But Rabbi, I'm only a visitor here." To which the rabbi answers, "So am I." While at first the rabbi may seem to be an ascetic, he's really not. His small home is, after all, filled with books. The rabbi doesn't have furniture because furniture isn't important to him, even if it is important to others. He has thousands of books, however, because they are important to him. Books, not furniture, give him pleasure.

Rather than renouncing the pursuit of all material possessions, we should renounce comparing ourselves to others and focus on what gives us pleasure. Take out your journal and turn to a blank page. Title it "Joys." Start listing all the things and activities that bring you joy. Once you find yourself struggling to come up with more items, put your journal down for a minute. Close your eyes, take one deep breath, and go back and read your list.

Do you enjoy having a house full of books, as did Rabbi Hayyim? Then by all means keep stacking them in every corner at the expense of having as much furniture as your neighbors. Does traveling to Europe every six months mean more to you than buying a home like all your peers? Pack your bags. Does becoming a carpenter mean more to you than being a professional like both your siblings? Take up your coping saw. Does being able to see all your daughter's dance recitals mean more to you than becoming vice president at the firm? Don't work late. Be true to yourself, and you'll find you're just where you're supposed to be . . . and you'll be happy.

"How Come She Got the Promotion?"

That's what Debbie Lewis desperately wants to know.

Debbie, forty-five, is a graphic designer who works for a midsize public relations and communications firm in New York City. Debbie, a petite woman with a head of tight red curls, is very good at what she does. She's creative, hardworking, and dependable. Yet for years she has been comparing and measuring her own career with that of her friend Randy Kaplan, forty-three.

Randy and Debbie both started working for the firm at about the same time, at the same level. Debbie's work was always of a higher quality than Randy's by any objective measure, yet Randy was the one who climbed the ladder faster. Earlier this year Randy was named head of the department, and the promotion really got to Debbie. Her anger at what she perceived to be an injustice had an impact on her relationship with Randy, which had previously been good. Debbie could sense her work was beginning to suffer.

After a couple of months of "venting" to her husband, Mitch, he decided to have a serious chat with her. Mitch asked Debbie about the differences between her and Randy. Debbie explained that while Randy's work was good, her own was better. "What about office politics?" Mitch asked. Debbie explained that while she was never a backstabber or manipulator, Randy spent a great deal more time politicking than she did. Randy was single and lived in the city, not far from the firm's offices. Debbie and Mitch had two children and lived in the suburbs, about an hour's train ride from the office. As a result, Debbie liked to leave the office at closing time, while Randy often stayed late. If there was deadline pressure, Debbie took work home, while Randy came into the office on weekends. In addition, Randy was always willing to travel on business, while Debbie was loath to spent extra time away from her husband and kids. Randy enjoyed going to industry conferences and meetings; it was a big part of her social life. Debbie, on the other hand, spent off hours with her and Mitch's extended families and friends from their hometown.

The more Debbie talked about the differences between her "work style" and Randy's "work style," the more she realized that while she "worked to live," Randy clearly "lived to work." Mitch asked if she would trade her life for Randy's. Did she want to stay late at the office and go in on weekends? Did she want to travel more on business? Did she want her social life to revolve more around her career? Debbie immediately said no to each question.

We spend our time envying people whom we wouldn't wish to be.

—Jean Rostand

Debbie's story reminds me of something the French author Jean Rostand once wrote: "We spend our time envying people whom we wouldn't wish to be." Everything of value has a cost. Career and business success don't come without a price. Work successes are part of a balanced life equation; they come at the expense of something else. It could be something as concrete as time spent with family, or it could be something as abstract as self-respect. When you find yourself comparing your career or business success with someone else's, take out your journal. Write that person's name and achievement on one line. Stop for a minute and think about what he or she gave up to achieve it. Write your answer on the line under the achievement. Now, ask yourself if you'd make the same sacrifice. Everyone needs to decide on his or her own career and business trade-offs. Focus on the value of what you've kept, not what you could have gotten in exchange.

"I Wish I Could Retire Early, Like You"

That's what Peter Green, fifty-three, said to his pal David Andrews, fifty-six, over beers at the clubhouse of a golf course in the Mid-Atlantic city in which they live.

Peter is manager of one of a chain of local auto dealers. The six-foot-six-inch former high school basketball star is married, with two kids in college. His wife, Jenny, fifty-four, works doing accounts receivable for a medical practice. They own a Cape Cod in the suburbs. Although they've never been spendthrifts,

Peter and Jenny have fully funded their 401(k)s—but that's about all their savings. Their retirement money has been invested in a combination of stock index funds and conservative bond funds. Both their kids took out student loans for college, and the Greens took out a home equity line of credit to help with the college bills.

David Andrews has been a partner in a local accounting firm for almost thirty years. A stocky, balding fellow, David is married to Allison, fifty-five, an attorney who has her own practice. The Andrewses own a condominium near the center city that serves both as their home and as Allison's office. They have no children. A few years back, David and Allison sold their home in the suburbs and made enough to pay off their small mortgage balance and pay cash for their current condo. With two large incomes to work with and few debts, David and Allison are able to put away a large percentage of their income. The Andrewses also invested aggressively, and some of their stock picks paid off handsomely. They were lucky enough to sell their high-tech and telecommunications holdings before the stock market bubble burst. Since then, they've become much more conservative. The Andrewses recently decided they'd work for another two years, then sell their condo and retire early to the Gulf Coast, where they've always enjoyed vacationing.

When Peter expressed his envy, David just shook his head. "No really," Peter added, "I should have gotten into the market in a bigger way."

David kept on shaking his head. "Peter," he said softly, "if I had kids, I couldn't have taken the same risks."

One of the immutable laws of personal finance is that to achieve great rewards, you need to take great risks. If you find yourself jealous of someone else's financial life, grab your journal. Write the person's name and some characterization of their financial reward on one line. Once again, ask yourself about the risks they've taken to get that reward. Jot down your answer on the next line. Then think about whether you were, or are, in a position to prudently take the same risk or risks. Is your income stream as secure? Do you have as many years to recover from a potential loss? Do you have the same financial cushion? Do you have more present and future financial obligations? Sure, you're envious of the reward . . . but should you take the same risk? Everyone needs to make his or her own risk analysis. Focus on getting the best reward possible for the risk you're prudently able to assume, not for how much someone else was willing to risk.

"I Wish My Husband Were as Romantic as Ellen's"

That was Adrianne Turner's complaint to her mother over coffee on a recent visit. Adrianne, a forty-three-year-old elementary school teacher, has been married for eleven years to Jeremy, forty-six, a product manager for a computer hardware manufacturer. She's slightly overweight and dresses almost exclusively in clothes from L. L. Bean. Ellen Powell, Adrianne's thirty-two-year-old sister, has been married to Steve, thirty-two, for seven years. She's taller and thinner than Adrianne and looks as though she could be in an ad for The Gap.

Adrianne's comment was in response to hearing that Steve had just bought Ellen a lovely broach . . . for no apparent reason. Adrianne is always hearing about Steve's buying Ellen clothing or bringing home flowers. Her own husband seems to pale in comparison. It's not that Jeremy isn't thoughtful, it's just that he never seems to do the little romantic things that could make someone feel especially loved. Jeremy never forgets a birthday, anniversary, or Valentine's Day, but he tends to buy more practical gifts or presents that fit in with Adrianne's hobbies: gardening and cooking. Jeremy never surprises Adrianne with flowers, except when she plants the seed by coming right out and saying she'd love it if he'd bring her flowers.

Adrianne's mother, Paula, sixty-three, shook her head disapprovingly after Adrianne finished. "Jeremy is a wonderful husband," she said. "He works hard, helps with the kids, and always puts you first. He may not be perfect . . . but no one is."

The poet and philosopher Ralph Waldo Emerson once wrote, "There is a crack in everything God made, and not least of all, in each one of us." There's no such thing as the perfect child, the perfect parent, the perfect spouse, the perfect sibling, or the perfect friend. There's no perfect family, and there's no perfect marriage. Yet when we compare our personal lives to someone else's, or to some abstract ideal, we seem always to focus on how ours don't measure up. There's a painfully funny moment in an episode of *Seinfeld*° in which George Costanza's father, Frank, played by Jerry Stiller, explains the family's celebration of their unique holiday, Festivus, rather than Christmas. One of the things the Costanzas do is go around the table as each family member tells the others how they've disappointed him or her during the past year. The Costanzas may be as dysfunctional as a family can get, but they provide a wonderful example . . . of what not to do.

> There is a crack in everything God made, and not least of all, in each one of us.
>
> —Ralph Waldo Emerson

°Created by Jerry Seinfeld and Larry David.

Instead of fixating on the minutiae in your personal life and how each individual aspect compares with those of the lives of others, focus on the big picture. Rather than going through a line-by-line analysis in your journal, write the name of the person in question on one line. Look at it. Visualize the person's face. Does this person bring you joy? Does this relationship add to your life? Forget about the checklists you see in *Cosmo* or *Brides*. How can you compare your child to other children or your wife to other wives? They are all unique individuals. And since you too are a unique individual, your relationships and family are unlike any other. Just as you should compare yourself only to yourself, you should compare your personal relationships only to your personal relationships. Are you as a couple, as a family, as friends, being true to your distinctive dynamic? That's the only yardstick that matters.

The Final Question

Let me finish this chapter with another story. One day the famous Hasidic rabbi Zyusa of Anapol comes staggering into the school where his followers gather. His eyes are red from crying, and his face is pale.

"Rabbi, you look frightened—what's wrong?" one of his followers asks.

"Last night I had a vision," Rabbi Zyusa explains. "In it I learned the question the angels will one day ask me about my life. And it terrified me."

His followers jump to comfort him. "Rabbi, you are pious, scholarly, and humble. You're a leader. You've helped hundreds of people. You've been a shepherd to your community. What question could the angels possibly ask about your life that would be so frightening to answer?"

Rabbi Zyusa doesn't seem to hear the intended words of comfort. Instead he lifts his gaze upward and says, "I've learned the angels will not ask me, 'Why weren't you a Moses, leading your people out of slavery?'"

One follower, enthralled, blurts out, "So what did they ask you?"

Still Rabbi Zyusa stares upward as if in a trance. "I've learned the angels will not ask me, 'Why weren't you a Joshua, leading your people into the promised land?'"

The most senior of the followers comes over to the rabbi and clutches his arm to break the spell. Zyusa lowers his gaze and looks at his devotee. "Rabbi, what is it the angels will ask you?" asks the devotee.

The rabbi begins to speak plaintively: "The angels will say to me: 'Zyusa, there was only one thing that no power of heaven or earth could have prevented you from becoming.' They will ask, 'Zyusa, why weren't you Zyusa?'"

God wants nothing more from the rest of us than he wants from Zyusa: to realize we are incomparable.

You're Just Where You're Supposed to Be

- We compare ourselves to others in dozens of ways, from the sublime to the ridiculous: how much we earn, the size of our homes, the cost of our cars, the extent of our social lives, our appearance, and many others.
- We're taught this behavior by our parents, who are pressured into it by a society that for better or worse uses economic, material, and external factors as yardsticks.
- Comparing ourselves to others will, little by little, year by year, destroy our chances for happiness in life. It's a race we can never win.

- Instead, we need to pursue those things that bring us pleasure, not the things others pursue or things we think should make us happy.
- We need to base decisions on our own lives, the lives we want to lead, not other people's lives or the lives others think we should lead.
- God wants us to realize we are all incomparable.

(3)

IT GETS BETTER

To be seventy years young is sometimes far
more cheerful and hopeful than to be forty
years old.
                                    —*Oliver Wendell Holmes Sr.*

Are there days you look around at your life, measure your
reality against your expectations, sigh, and think to yourself, This is as good as it gets? It's not; it gets better.

Every life has a tipping point. For most of us, that moment
comes between the ages of forty and sixty, in the period called
"middle age."

Up until this point you're hopeful, optimistic, and enthusiastic. You see your life as one of progress and improvement. Sure,
you have setbacks in your career, but in general you're climbing
the ladder, boosting your income, growing your business,
and/or improving your skills. Perhaps your personal life isn't going completely according to plan, but you have family and
friends who love and care for you. Maybe you're not a million-

aire, but odds are you can put food on the table, keep a roof over your head, and take a vacation now and then. Then something happens.

One morning you wake up with a backache after spending the day before on the golf course. Yes, you were able to play thirty-six holes—play them pretty well, actually—but you're paying for it now. Or you come home from your yearly physical with a handful of prescriptions. Sure, they're "preventive"— maybe to lower your slightly elevated cholesterol and blood pressure—but you're suddenly having to pay attention to drug interactions. It could be you notice the new vice president of your division is a couple of years younger than you. Maybe you're updating your résumé and realize you've nothing new to add to your list of achievements. Perhaps it's some innocuous little observation: an attractive young waitperson treats your flirtatiousness with condescension rather than annoyance or interest; or you discover hair sprouting in new places and falling out of others.

Actually, it's probably not just one observation or incident, but a series or accumulation. What matters is that your attitude toward life shifts. Instead of being hopeful, maybe you start feeling depressed. Perhaps you begin thinking your life isn't going anywhere, that you've peaked and are heading downhill. It could be you stop looking for ways to improve yourself and your life. You may make all the right noises about "staying active and engaged," but inside you downshift, pull over into the slow lane, and start looking for the exit ramp. You stop looking at time as a positive force and start seeing it negatively. You stop looking forward to the rest of your life, eagerly anticipating tomorrow, and instead start looking backward, afraid of what the future holds. You view the day as something to endure rather than enjoy. The hours drag by rather than fly by.

Alan Cohen, forty-three, feels beaten. For the past fifteen

years, the youthful-looking Alan has been managing one of the largest independent liquor stores in the Northeast. In that time, Alan has helped boost the store's reputation so that some customers now drive for more than an hour to browse and buy at the suburban store. Alan and his wife, Cheryl, have a sixteen-year-old daughter and a twelve-year-old son. The family owns a split-level house about thirty minutes from the store. Cheryl works part-time doing clerical work in a dental office. While the Cohens aren't affluent, they've never felt they lacked for anything. But recently Alan has become worried. The owner of the store has been spending less and less time there. A seventy-year-old former police officer, he has always been generous to Alan and his family. But it's becoming clear he doesn't intend to hold on to the store for much longer.

Alan can't afford to buy the store, and the owner can't afford not to get top dollar for it—he's counting on the sale of the store to fund his retirement. Alan sees his stream of income and economic future vanishing before his eyes. His daughter is an excellent student who's planning to apply to Ivy League colleges. His son has a severe allergy that requires expensive medications and treatments. Cheryl's job provides enough money only for vacations and holidays, and even if she worked full-time, she probably wouldn't pull in much more. Alan thinks he's a failure. Just when he most needs to provide for his family, it looks as though he won't be able to. He's convinced his only hope is to ingratiate himself with the new owners of the store, whoever they might be, and for all family members to tighten their belts.

Alan doesn't need to feel this way. And neither do you if you're in a similar situation. The tipping point of your life doesn't need to be a harmful moment when you shift from optimism to pessimism, from hope to resignation, from enthusiasm to complacency. It can be a positive moment, a second birth, a reinvigoration, a rekindling of dreams. It can be a chance for you to reenergize your pursuit of tomorrow. All you need is the right attitude about time.

The Passage of Time

The attitude you need to adopt to insure that the spark of life remains vibrant, to be happy today, is simple: It gets better. The simple passage of time enhances your life. Keep breathing and your life will improve.

The simple passage of time enhances your life. Keep breathing and your life will improve.

Julius Caesar said, "Experience is the teacher of all things." Miguel de Cervantes echoed that, writing, "Time ripens all things. No man is born wise." Both men realized the longer you live, the more experiences you gather and, as a result, the more you learn. It doesn't matter whether or not you immediately overcome every obstacle you face. You learn just as much, if not more, through failure as you do through success. Learning what doesn't work is still learning. As time passes, experience becomes wisdom. You may not be able to work eighteen hours a day, as you did when you first started your career. But now you don't need to work eighteen hours a day to get the job done. You work smarter rather than longer, and as a result, you get more accomplished in less time with fewer mistakes.

That's certainly the case with Daniel Cantor, seventy-two, who feels he hasn't yet hit his prime as an attorney. While the thin, gray-haired Daniel comes into the office at 10:00 a.m., takes a nap every afternoon from 1:00 to 2:00 p.m., and leaves by 4:00 p.m., he's billing more money than ever before. A specialist in business acquisition, Daniel has years of experience that enable him to quickly zero in on the strengths and weaknesses of any business that's up for sale. He's renowned for being able to close complex negotiations in a single session. Daniel's reputation is such that even after raising his fees dramatically, he's still turning down clients.

Time doesn't just add wisdom, it takes away suffering too. Benjamin Disraeli called time "the great physician," playing on the old saying that time heals all wounds. As time passes, injuries you've suffered, whether physical, emotional, or psychological, become less painful. Sure, there may still be a scar or a soreness, but the pain isn't as intense or potentially debilitating. Broken hearts mend. The death of a loved one never leaves us, and there's always a missing piece in our lives. The dissolution of a serious relationship cuts deeply. But the passage of time helps shift focus from the negative to the positive. The more time passes, the more time you spend thinking about the good years and the less time you spend thinking about the final days.

Bernice Sitney, fifty-three, thought she'd never get over the death of her daughter, Tina, at age ten from leukemia. But twenty years later, she's never seen without her makeup on and her hair just right and she finds herself thinking more about the ten years of joy that Tina gave her than the pain of those final few months. Tina's death and Bernice's subsequent divorce led her to go back to school to study social work. For the past ten years, she has been working with hospital patients and their families.

Thomas Jefferson suggested, "When angry, count ten before you speak; if very angry, an hundred." Jefferson's advice works because anger drains away as time passes. In the short term, just taking a breath and allowing the initial "fight or flight" reflex to subside helps overcome anger. The English have a lovely way of encouraging this kind of pause. They say, "You're never too busy for a cup of tea." While their teatime is not as ritualized as the Japanese tea ceremony, the English will take time out in the midst of a crisis, whether personal or professional, brew a "proper cup" of tea, and then sip it calmly. The enforced break almost always allows calmer heads to prevail.

Diane Milton, a pale twenty-seven-year-old with maroon hair, hates dealing with bureaucracies, particularly insurance companies. When she received notification from her health insurance provider that it wouldn't cover the Botox injections she's getting for her severe migraines, she dreaded making the appeal telephone call. Her fears were realized when she found herself talking to a less than sympathetic or helpful person. Rather than getting angry, yelling at the insurance company employee, hanging up the telephone, and probably giving herself a migraine, she took a deep breath and asked to speak to a supervisor.

Looking back, Mark Twain saw that time helped put even profound issues in perspective. "When I was a boy of fourteen," he wrote, "my father was so ignorant I could hardly stand to have the old man around. But when I got to be twenty-one, I was astonished at how much he had learned in seven years." At the age of twenty you might be hurt and unforgiving about your father's failure to attend any of your lacrosse games in high school. By the age of fifty you may not have forgotten the slights, but you've forgiven the old man. As you age and come face-to-face with your own shortcomings, it's easier to overlook the shortcomings of others. The French philosopher Blaise Pascal wrote, "Time heals grief and quarrels, for we change and are no longer the same persons. Neither the offender nor the offended are any more themselves."

> Time heals grief and quarrels, for we change and are no longer the same persons. Neither the offender nor the offended are any more themselves.
>
> —Blaise Pascal

Tim Stone, thirty-eight, has been angry with his identical twin brother, James, for close to ten years. When their parents' newsstand business started going under and their mother, who ran it alone after their father's death, asked for help, James did nothing. Tim was left having to help his mother close up. But with their mother's sixty-fifth birthday party rapidly approaching, Tim is ready to deal with James. Now that Tim has just had his first child, he has a new appreciation for what James was going through. At the time of the store's collapse, James's wife had just given birth. Tim hasn't forgotten the past, but he feels he can put it behind him.

The older we get, the wider our perspective on the world. Think about how long the summer felt when you were in junior high school. You could become "best friends" with someone you'd never met before. "Romances" could begin, flourish, and fade all in the space of two months. Each day, each week, and each month seemed to go on forever. Now fast-forward to today. Think about how quickly the summers pass. You never get around to buying and planting those perennials because you're too busy. The two-week vacation flies by in what seems like less time than it took to plan. You barely scratch off a couple of things on your to-do list or get started on that stack of "beach books" before it's time to put the sandals away.

"Happiness may well consist primarily of an attitude toward time," wrote the author Robert Grudin. I couldn't agree more. The younger you are, the higher the percentage of your total life each day makes up, so the higher percentage of your total life experience each mistake or disappointment represents. The longer you live, the less impact each incident can have on your life. Experience brings wisdom and happiness. Time heals wounds. Anger fades. As long as you keep living, keep moving forward, your life gets better and you grow happier.

Time Is a River

I also agree with Marcus Aurelius, who wrote, "Time is a sort of river of passing events." I believe time flows through our lives bringing joys, not sorrows, bringing opportunities, not crises. It's a positive force that we can ride to happiness, if only we let ourselves be carried by its currents. You can choose to ride the positive river flowing through life or you can choose to fight the current and struggle to stay in place.

You can choose to ride the positive river flowing through life or you can choose to fight the current and struggle to stay in place.

Try to fight the passage of time and what happens? You become an object of derision, pity, and scorn. There's nothing wrong with staying in shape. Exercise and healthy living will help you stay alive and fully able to engage in life. You will look and feel great . . . for your age. Trying to look younger than you are, on the other hand, is problematic. Surgical efforts to turn back the clock, for instance, are usually obvious to everyone other than the patient. There's also nothing wrong with staying abreast of the latest trends in fashion. Being stylish has nothing to do with age. But dressing like a twentysomething when you're fifty is pitiful. By all means, do everything you can to feel and look as good as you can. Just don't try to pretend you're not your age. Buying a BMW roadster doesn't cut twenty years off a sixty-five–year–old man's age; it just makes him look desperate. It's an outward expression of an inner unease with who and what he is.

One of the most entertaining portrayals of this effort to recapture lost youth comes in the William Dean Howells novel *Indian Summer*. Theodore Colville, a successful newspaper publisher in the Midwest, feels that his life has passed him by. He decides to sell his business and head back to Italy, where as a young man he dreamed of becoming an architect and had a tragic love affair.

A wonderful recent example of this desperation is in the film *American Beauty*.* Lester Burnham, played by Kevin Spacey, feels he is a loser in a dead-end job, in a loveless marriage, and with an uncaring daughter. One night his wife, played by Annette Bening, drags him to see his daughter's cheerleading squad. There, Lester falls madly in love with one of his daughter's friends, who seems to personify the youth and vibrancy he has lost. Lester quits his job, buys a sports car, starts lifting weights and taking drugs—all ostensibly to win the young girl, but actually to feel alive again.

Don't try to turn back the hands of time. Accept yourself and embrace the passage of time. You are better today than you were yesterday, and you will be better yet tomorrow. You may not have the body of a twenty–year–old, but your experience makes you a better lover. You may have lines on your face, but they give you character and signal wisdom. You may not be able to work twelve-hour days . . . but you don't need to. You may not be proficient at day-trading stocks online, but you're savvy enough to know you can't time the market.

Whether or not you embrace the passage of time, you will

*Directed by Sam Mendes and written by Alan Ball.

end up in the same place. Every human being suffers from a fatal disease: life. No matter how much money and effort you spend trying to hold back the clock, it will move ahead. You can no more stop the hands of time from turning than you can stop a mighty river from flowing. You can try to dam or divert it, but it will flow somewhere. Time will pass—your children will leave the nest, you will develop wrinkles, loved ones will die—no matter what you do. We are mortals. "Do not try to live forever," advised George Bernard Shaw. "You will not succeed."

While we're all destined to end up in the same place, we do have a choice as to what our journey will be like. If you think your life is half-over, you'll spend the rest of it being miserable or trying desperately to regain your youth. If you think your career has peaked, you'll spend the rest of your working years chasing the past or doing nothing of consequence. If you think you've been a financial failure, you'll forever focus on what you lack rather than what you have. If you let time become your enemy, you'll spend the rest of your life either in the past or just waiting to die.

Sam van Pelt, thirty-four, is clearly living in the past. As a young man growing up in a small Minnesota town, Sam was the local hockey hero. After leading his high school to the state championship, Sam went on to star in college and then made it to the National Hockey League. Sam was building a solid hockey career for himself until he suffered a series of concussions. Told by his doctor that playing any longer would lead to permanent brain damage, Sam had to hang up his skates at age twenty-nine. Since that tipping point, Sam hasn't been able to move ahead. He returned to his old hometown, bought a bar, filled it with his hockey memorabilia, and now holds court every day and night. Sam tells the same old stories to the same people night after night.

You don't have to end up stuck in the past, like Sam. If you embrace time, if you adopt the attitude that the passage of time is wonderful, your life will improve. If you think your career will keep improving, you'll look forward to work each morning. If you feel your financial life will keep getting better you'll relish all you do have. If you keep looking forward to tomorrow, every day you're alive will be better than the day before. View the passage of time positively and you'll even make death a non-event; you'll spend your life actually living rather than just surviving. Michel de Montaigne wrote, "I want Death to find me planting my cabbages, neither worrying about it nor the unfinished gardening."

> View the passage of time positively and you'll even make death a non-event; you'll spend your life actually living rather than just surviving.

Laura Bennett, forty-seven, looks forward to each morning. Seven years ago, just after her fortieth birthday, the painfully thin brunette was diagnosed with breast cancer. After a mastectomy and a long course of chemotherapy, Laura got a clean bill of health. A successful marketing executive, Laura was unattached at the time. She had her share of dark days and even darker nights. There were moments she beat herself up over having put her career first. There were other times she wanted to give up finding anyone with whom to share her life. But she resolved to look forward and regain her optimism. Although she's still single, she is currently involved in a long-term relationship and is training to compete in a triathlon.

I have a great deal of admiration for people like Laura. I realize how hard it can sometimes be to see that life gets better. In the past few years, I've buried my mother, my younger brother, my younger sister, and, as I was writing this book, my father. I now find myself the last of my immediate family. I've seen one of my daughters and sons-in-law forced to deal with chronic disease. Don't get me wrong. I'm not writing this in an effort to prompt sympathy. Nor am I looking to top any reader's litany of woes. I just want to point out that, like everyone else, I've had to deal with sadness. But despite these events, I have faith life gets better. No—it's not that I have faith life gets better, I *know* life gets better. I see it every day. I see how Mark's writing and my consulting work keep improving. I see how my friendships deepen. I see how my love for my wife grows more profound. I see how my pride in my children continues to soar. And I see how my grandchildren blossom. I choose to see how my life gets better. And that makes all the difference.

You have a choice in how you view the world. You can focus on injustice and sadness and misery, or you can focus on justice, happiness, and joy. There's a wonderful story about two friends facing this choice. It originally appeared in the 1950s as a short story entitled "My War with Hersh Rasseyner," written by Chaim Grade. Since then it has been adopted into a play and a short film. The three works vary somewhat but essentially tell the same story. One day a successful writer named Chaim is walking through a park in a city he's visiting. He sees a familiar face. Chaim is overjoyed to realize the familiar face is his childhood friend Hersh. Both men grew up in pre–World War II Poland. They were students in the same yeshiva. Both were caught up in the Holocaust and lost all their families and, they thought, all their friends as well. After reveling in their joint survival, the two begin to debate their different reactions to the circumstances of their lives: Chaim's reaction has been to become an agnostic, while Hersh's response has been to grow even more devout.

Thank God the choice most of us face isn't as stark as that which faced Chaim and Hersh in the story. But like them, you have a choice. You can believe time is a negative force you must battle or a positive force making your life better. You can focus on your death or you can focus on your life.

Taking Baby Steps

Even putting the choice in such stark terms, I know it's not easy. It's hard to change your attitude toward time. Isaac Newton wrote that a body at rest tends to remain at rest and that a body in motion tends to remain in motion. If you've spent years being depressed, sitting on the shore rather than riding the positive river of time, you're like a body at rest; it will take some effort to get you moving. The good news is that once you start moving, you'll tap into the flow and pick up speed; you'll be like a body in motion. The secret is to take some baby steps out into the river to get you thinking and acting positively.

Pick an area or aspect of your life about which you're feeling negative. Say, your career. Take out your journal and turn to a blank page. Title the page "Negative Trends." Start writing down what about your life is making you feel negative. For example, if you feel your income isn't increasing as quickly as it should, write that down. If you think you've been passed over for promotion, note that as well. The idea is to take an abstract problem and make it concrete. Take each of the concrete examples you've written and give them a bit of thought. Set down your journal and do something to free up your mind, like taking a walk.

When you next get a chance, pick up your journal again. Turn back to "Negative Trends." Turn to the next blank page and title it "Turnarounds." Write a series of solutions to the problems you listed on the "Negative Trends" page. Let's go back to the sense that you're not earning enough salary. The solutions you write down might include Ask for a raise; Look for a new job; Consider a career change; Get a second job; and/or Start a business.

Now, take each solution and give it a separate page in your journal. On those pages, break down each solution into a series of specific small steps. For example, if you're considering asking for a raise, you might come up with a list like Research industry salary range; Develop list of accomplishments and contributions; Prepare pitch memo; Determine best time for approach; Make appointment with supervisor.

Having done this with each of your potential solutions, pick which one you think is the most appropriate choice. Then start working on the first baby step.

"I'm Afraid of Having Another Heart Attack"

Bob Dietrich, forty-nine, first felt the chest pain when he was washing the dishes after dinner. He, his wife, Karen, and their son, Eric, fourteen, had just finished a lovely meal and were getting ready to sit down together to watch *The Sopranos*. Bob initially thought it was indigestion. But when it didn't go away, his arm started getting numb, and he began to break out into a sweat, he started getting nervous. So did Karen. She hustled Bob and Eric into their car and drove right to the hospital, calling on her cell phone while driving to tell the emergency room they were on the way. It was a good thing she acted so quickly. It turned out Bob was in the initial stages of a heart attack. Luckily for them all, Bob's wasn't a major coronary. The doctors told Bob his heart would recover with medical support and lifestyle changes. That turned out to be true for Bob's physical health; his mental health was something different.

Bob had always been an avid golfer, and he, Eric, and Karen

were committed hikers. One of the family's little rituals was to plan future trips and adventures. They went over tour books together and figure out itineraries. Before his heart attack, Bob and Karen had a good sex life. But despite his doctor's encouragement, six months after his heart attack, Bob was still frightened of doing anything strenuous. He spent most of his spare time watching television or reading. In their own ways, both Karen and Eric tried to bring back "the old Bob." Bob, however, just joked sadly that "old" was the right word for him and refused to stir. His golfing buddies tried to get him back out on the links, joking that he now gave them all a good excuse to use carts. But Bob just laughed and didn't take them up on the offer. It wasn't until Karen and Eric began planning a hiking trip of their own to Scotland that a light bulb went off over Bob's head. His family and friends were going to move ahead with or without him, so he had a choice.

The next weekend, Bob sat down early Sunday morning with a legal pad. He had decided the best thing he could do to improve his mental health and restore his optimism was to get physically active again. He began drawing up a step-by-step program for himself, starting with nightly walks around the neighborhood along with Karen and sessions at the driving range with a couple of his buddies. Bob drew up a list of his fears and tried to come up with solutions. For instance, he decided to buy a heart rate monitor with sound alerts that he could wear while exercising. He also decided to get a set of instant connect cell phones for the family so they could quickly get in touch.

After just a week on his new program, the change in Bob's attitude was dramatic. While he's still not yet confident enough to go on a long-distance hike with Karen and Eric, they're all planning a trip to the Scottish Highlands for next year. And although he's not up to playing eighteen holes yet, he is driving the cart for the rest of his foursome and taking the occasional swing.

"My Career Is Over"

Sarah Jefferson, forty-two, has carved out a wonderful career. An attractive, fashionable, single woman, she works as a curator at one of the nation's most prestigious art museums. For years, Sarah's self-image has been of the young go-getter at the museum and one of the trendsetters in the industry. She prides herself on bringing innovation and a fresh approach to what is known as a very traditional institution. That's why Sarah was so upset to learn about her new boss. The new curatorial director is a thirty-four-year-old woman who has made a name for herself running cutting-edge programs at another museum.

Sarah feels her career has come to a dead end. It is clear to her that the path up the ladder at this museum is now blocked by her new boss, who is not only younger than Sarah, but also has the same approach. At best, Sarah thinks she could become the new director's right-hand person. At the same time, Sarah feels she has few options at other museums. Shifting institutions would mean a loss of seniority, even if it didn't mean a cut in pay. That would put her further from the top than ever. In addition, she would then be competing with even more people younger than her. Sarah feels as though her work life is over: she isn't just a "has-been," she is a "never-was."

What has made the situation even harder for Sarah is that her work life and personal life are closely linked. Since so much of her job involves meeting with artists, gallery owners, and collectors, most of her "spare time" is spent at social events in the evening and on weekends. Vacations are usually working trips to other museums or visits to art shows. Most of Sarah's friends are involved in the art world as well.

When Sarah decided her career had ended, she retreated not just at work, but at home as well. She stopped going to as many events, stopped socializing as much. Of course, spending time alone at home made her even more depressed.

One evening, Sarah came home from work and went through her mail as she usually did. She found what looked like a wedding invitation. The sight of it started a spiral into depression. Still, she opened it and discovered that while it was indeed an invitation, it was to a memorial service rather than a wedding—a memorial service for her. The RSVP contact was the telephone number of her best friend, a performance artist she met when they were both fresh out of college. Sarah got the message. She called her friend and apologized for not being in touch for so long. As she explained the situation at work, she was surprised to find her friend giving her no sympathy; instead, he chastised her, telling her to start "thinking outside the box" and then going on to talk about the projects he was working on.

After the conversation, Sarah hung up the telephone, poured herself a glass of wine, and started thinking about her friend's reaction. She decided to do something about her situation. She took out her journal and began making notes about her problems. Sarah determined that her friend might be right. Maybe her major problem was that she was stuck in her thinking. Rather than thinking of other museum jobs, she started jotting down alternative fields in which her experience would be helpful. She wrote down art schools, art stores, art supply manufacturers, art galleries, and auction houses. The idea of working in a school, store, or corporate setting threatened to make her more depressed. But working for a gallery or auction house piqued her interest. Those options would provide the same kind of work/personal life interaction she enjoyed. The next day, she started making some telephone calls.

As this book goes to press, Sarah is still working at the museum, but she has turned down one job offer from a gallery and is in negotiation with an auction house over another offer. Her spark has returned, she is back socializing, and she is talking enthusiastically about working at the auction house.

"My Dreams for Retirement Are Shattered"

Edith Lefkowitz, sixty-four, feels her dream is shattered. Widowed in her early fifties, the rosy-cheeked, gray-haired Edith has been working as an office manager for more than ten years. Her late husband left her with a small pension, and together they were able to put aside some money over the years. Having just become vested in her own pension program at work, Edith was planning on retiring next year. Her dream was to sell her home in the suburbs of a major northeastern city, invest the proceeds, and live off her pension incomes, Social Security, and interest. To stretch her money and improve her quality of life, Edith intended to move south to a Sunbelt state. In order to help with all the planning, Edith met with a financial planner. It was then she reached her own tipping point.

The financial planner thought Edith's ideas were fine. He went over her savings and investments, her projected pension and Social Security incomes, her home's market value, and the costs of buying an apartment down south. He explained to Edith that her plan was certainly doable, as long as she invested in securities that generated sufficient income. That meant being a bit more aggressive.

The word "aggressive" set off alarm bells in Edith's head. Since the death of her husband, Edith had been very conservative. When her friends jokingly called her cheap, she responded by saying she preferred the word "frugal." Edith's savings were all in certificates of deposit and Treasury bonds. Edith realized that although more aggressive investments could mean better income, they could also mean less income or, worse, a loss of principal. Having done without to save the money, she hated risking any loss.

Patiently, the financial planner went over all his numbers again and explained that Edith needed to generate more income to fully retire and live the life she dreamed. Edith told him she had to think it over.

For the next two months, Edith was in a funk. Her friends said they hadn't seen her this low since the death of her husband. She dramatically told them she felt as if she were going through another death, this time of her dreams of retirement. One of Edith's friends suggested Edith speak with her daughter, who was a financial adviser. Although Edith didn't think it would make a difference, she agreed.

The second financial adviser echoed the advice of the first. But she also noted that Edith needed to do something not just for her financial well-being, but for her emotional well-being too. There's a difference between living and just existing, and Edith, the adviser suggested, needed to take steps to feel better. Her idea was for Edith to suspend but not abandon the idea of immediate retirement at sixty-five. That would take the time pressure off. Instead, she urged Edith to make some minor changes in her investment portfolio. The adviser told Edith that when certificates and bonds came due, she should look to put the money in some relatively safe mutual funds. The adviser also suggested that Edith look into buying rather than renting a place in the Sunbelt. If she paid for the apartment outright, using some of the proceeds from the sale of her home, she could lower her need for monthly income and perhaps provide herself with a greater sense of security.

Today Edith is following the second adviser's ideas, slowly shifting her savings pattern. She's still working as an office manager and has made some trips south to look at condominiums for sale in retirement communities. While her initial investments haven't all gone up, she's sensing she could weather the occasional downturn in the stock market. She'll never become an aggressive investor, but she's feeling better about her future than she has in months.

I know the stories of Bob, Sarah, and Edith make this process seem simple. That's because while the problem is complex, the solution is simple. The idea is to give yourself a series of easily accomplished baby steps to get you moving in a positive direction. Each time you tackle and complete one of the baby steps, you gain momentum. Remember, time is a positive force, and as you gain momentum you tap deeper into this positive flow. It's not just you doing the work; there's an incredibly powerful force helping you move in the right direction. By the time you finish one or two projects, your attitude will have changed for the better. Complete a few more projects and your attitude will again improve. Soon you will be living a hopeful, optimistic, enthusiastic life. It's just a matter of time.

Think of Scarlett O'Hara at the end of *Gone With the Wind*.° She has seen her daughter die. Finally free to marry Ashley Wilkes, the man she thought was her true love, he rejects her. She realizes too late that she has lost the one man she truly loved, Rhett Butler. Yet Scarlett chooses to look on the passage of time as positive. She remains optimistic. She's still hopeful. The book ends with an affirmation: "After all, tomorrow is another day."

°Written by Margaret Mitchell.

It Gets Better

- We let tipping points in our lives shift our attitude from hopeful to depressed, from optimistic to pessimistic.
- Cultivate the attitude that the passage of time is a positive force in your life, not a negative force.
- Time leads to wisdom and happiness.
- Time eases pain.
- Time lessens anger.
- Time adds perspective.
- Fight against time and your life will get worse; embrace the passage of time and your life will improve and you'll be happy.
- Start taking small, simple, concrete steps in the direction you want and you'll find your attitude changing.

(4)

OWN YOUR SUCCESS

We have to learn to be our own best friends because we fall too easily into the trap of being
our worst enemies.

—*Roderick Thorp*

P lease stop beating yourself up, focusing on what you did
wrong, highlighting your faults. You are an estimable person, deserving of praise and admiration. Your successes
aren't accidents, and your qualities aren't negligible.

When faced with facts that show you to be an estimable person, do you ignore them and invent failings or excavate obscure
flaws to deflect the praise? If you're like most of us, you do
things to yourself you'd never let others get away with and
think things about yourself you'd never let others say without
challenge. In the process, you damage your self-esteem in ways
your most obnoxious critic could never achieve, and you ensure
your unhappiness.

If you're like most of us, you do things to yourself you'd never let others get away with and think things about yourself you'd never let others say without challenge.

Think I'm exaggerating? How do you react when someone pays you a compliment? Do you simply say, "Thank you," and take ownership of your own success and your positive traits, or do you reflexively belittle your achievements or qualities? Maybe you say, "It was nothing." Perhaps you respond, "Anyone could have done it." Even worse, you may contradict, saying, "I really wasn't that good," or, "I could have done much better." On the surface, these responses seem like relatively minor instances of self-deprecation. But I think they're outward symbols of something very damaging. Most times, these public statements conceal even more withering internal comments. While you're saying, "Anyone could have done it," you may be thinking, I've fooled them again . . . I'm an imposter. You might be saying, "It was really nothing," and inside thinking, They don't know I'm really a terrible person. It's amazing how brutal and harmful we can be to ourselves.

I'm as guilty of this as anyone I know. Throughout my entire life and career, I've been unable to own my successes. The moment I achieved a goal, won an award, or received an accolade, it no longer was important or valuable. I had already moved on to the next goal, award, or accolade. Forget about giving myself a momentary pat on the back, I couldn't accept praise even from others. Outwardly I'd credit someone else or outside circumstances, while inwardly I'd criticize myself for not doing more sooner. For instance, I have four wonderful, high-achieving children, who have all married four equally wonderful, high-achieving people. Many times people complimented me on my parenting success, asking for my secret. Invariably, I used to respond, "Don't ask me, I wasn't there. Ask my wife, Corky." Sure, there was a kernel of truth to this. For much of my life, I was a workaholic. Still, as I've come to admit, I did play a positive role in raising my children. Now I try to take pride in that.

Real-World Success Doesn't Matter

The discrepancy between the external reality of people's lives and how they view themselves is often extreme. Wealth doesn't matter. I've met very affluent people who, inside their own heads, see themselves as failures. Notoriety doesn't matter. I know lots of famous people who see themselves as losers. Even people who've succeeded in incredibly competitive artistic spheres denigrate themselves. Take Pattie Townsend.

A forty-five-year-old party planner, Pattie had grown tired of arranging other people's weddings. Ever since she was a little girl, Pattie had loved taking photographs, particularly of people. She always enjoyed speaking with the photographers at the affairs she planned. In her spare time, she started researching the art photo market and developing some ideas. After only two years, Pattie was able to get a one-woman show of her photos at a local gallery. It was a critical success, and sales were beyond expectations. The gallery was so pleased, it offered Pattie a follow-up show months later. At the second show, sales were even better than at the first, and it was met with just as much acclaim. When last I spoke with her, the third show was just being assembled, but there was already buzz about it. In response, the gallery wanted to sign her to a long-term contract. Yet Pattie refuses to own any of this success. "Anyone could do it," she says when someone offers congratulations. When pressed she says, "They're just snapshots . . . its not like I'm Diane Arbus." And when close friends keep pressing further, she finally says, "I could make more money bagging groceries." I'm sure her internal monologue is even more disparaging. It seems no amount of external recognition can get Pattie to own her success.

Most people are amazed to find out they're not the only ones who beat themselves up like this. People are shocked to hear that wealthy businessmen, famous television personalities, and successful authors feel the same way. That's because we see the lives of others through the lens of reality, while we see our own lives through the lens of self-esteem or, more accurately, low self-esteem. The poet Henry Wadsworth Longfellow once wrote, "We judge ourselves by what we feel capable of doing, while others judge us by what we have already done." In other words, we measure others by real-world results, while we measure ourselves against the best potential outcome. It's as if a hockey goalie whose team has just won the Stanley Cup and who has been named the MVP of the playoffs criticizes himself because he could have done better: he could have had a shutout in every game.

> We judge ourselves by what we feel capable of doing, while others judge us by what we have already done.
> —Henry Wadsworth Longfellow

No amount of praise or compliments from others can make up for this unreal view of self. Franz Kafka is today regarded as one of the most influential authors of the twentieth century. And while he was working on his stories, showing them to other writers and friends in pre–World War II Czechoslovakia, they told him as much. Yet he published little in his lifetime, seemingly afraid to let much of his work see the light of day. Just before Kafka's early death, he made a dear friend, the writer Max

Brod, promise to burn all Kafka's unfinished and unpublished stories and novels. Luckily, Brod was able to see the quality of Kafka's work through the lens of reality and broke his promise.

Why do we do this to ourselves? According to psychologists, this kind of behavior is probably linked to some unresolved conflict we've had with an authority figure, often a parent. Maybe your mother told you she was disappointed you didn't put more effort into choosing a gift for your father, when actually you spent hours debating what to buy your old man. Alternatively, you might have been praised for what you knew to be a less than praiseworthy effort. Perhaps a coach held up your effort as an example to the rest of your Little League team, when in your heart you knew you hadn't given your all. Odds are it wasn't one such incident. Maybe you had a parent who could find the cloud around every silver lining or a series of teachers who let you coast through school. Whatever the cause, it's time to move on. I'll leave it to you to decide whether you need to have some kind of psychotherapeutic moment of confrontation. I'm not a therapist. All I can do is call you on your behavior and give you some ideas for getting over it.

Self-Criticism Versus Self-Denigration, and Humility Versus Pomposity

Many times, when I try to call people on their self-denigration, they respond by saying it's justifiable self-criticism. "The best way to improve or learn is to get unbiased opinions," they say in defense of beating themselves up.

They're right that self-criticism is a great tool for self-improvement. Reviewing past actions and results, analyzing what worked and what didn't, and then factoring the findings into your future behavior is a time-tested way to better yourself.

But many of us confuse self-denigration with self-criticism. When you're realistically assessing your successes as well as your failures, when you're patting yourself on the back as well as kicking yourself in the ass, and when you're keeping track of what you did well as well as what you did poorly, you're engaging in realistic self-criticism. When all you can see are your failures, when all you can do is beat yourself up, and when all you can focus on is how you came up short of the best possible result, you're engaging in irrational self-denigration.

Other times, I hear people defend their self-abuse by saying, "I don't want to blow my own horn." Well, there's a big difference between owning your success and being pompous. Pomposity is going out of your way to tout your successes, real or imagined, often at the expense of others. When offered a compliment, the pompous person pushes for even more compliments and, if they're not offered, provides them him- or herself. The pompous person doesn't own just *his* success, he's looking to take title to other people's successes as well.

"To teeter at the extremes of self-love and self-loathing, to pursue perfection because we despise our imperfection," wrote author Ernest Kurtz, "is to find neither satisfaction in successes nor wisdom in failures. Life becomes a constant battle, a never ending struggle to get somewhere, to achieve something, to produce something."

We need to own our successes as well as our failures. We need to be able to say thank you when we receive a compliment, just as easily as we apologize for a failing. We need to adopt an attitude of humility. Being humble means being honest with yourself; acknowledging your strengths and your weaknesses; owning your successes and your failures. Being humble doesn't mean thinking less of yourself, it means thinking less about yourself. According to the British author Henry Fairlie, "The foundation of humility is truth. The humble man," he wrote, "sees himself as he is. If his deprecation of himself were untrue, . . . it would not be praiseworthy, and would be a form of hypocrisy, which is one of the evils of Pride."

We need to own our successes as well as our failures. We need to be able to say thank you when we receive a compliment, just as easily as we apologize for a failing.

Later in this chapter, I'll offer some suggestions about how you can cultivate humility and learn to own your success. But first, let me explain why it's so important to get over this irrational self-criticism.

Owning Your Success Is Vital

To be happy, you need to own your success. A positive self-image will give you the confidence and faith to live life to the fullest. Your personal life, your career, and your finances will all flourish. As Oscar Wilde joked, "To love oneself is the beginning of a lifelong romance." On the other hand, when you denigrate yourself, you chip away at your self-esteem. Low self-esteem will affect your career, your finances, and your personal life. It will doom you to unhappiness. To paraphrase Wilde, to hate oneself is the beginning of lifelong animosity.

To love oneself is the beginning of a lifelong romance.
—Oscar Wilde

If you can't own your successes at work, you won't have the confidence to go after the new job that opens up in the home office, you'll be an ineffective advocate for a salary increase, and you won't be considered for plum assignments. If you're always finding fault with yourself, you'll be afraid of spending too much on your house, you'll worry obsessively over investments and probably overreact, and you'll never have the confidence to enjoy whatever wealth you do build up. When you're constantly beating yourself up, you won't have the self-assurance to try new things, to meet new people, or to take risks and follow your heart. Constantly denigrate yourself and you establish a pattern that leads to a life full of regrets. A lack of self-esteem narrows the world dramatically. Take it from me, no one, looking back on life from the perspective of seven or more decades, regrets taking too many risks; we regret not taking more.

Poet and playwright Edmond Rostand created a character whose self-denigration dooms him to a life less rewarding than it should have been. Cyrano de Bergerac is a famous swordsman and poet who lets his hatred of his own appearance keep him from the love of his life, the beautiful Roxane. Cyrano helps his handsome but vacuous friend Christian woo and win Roxane by providing him with poems and words of love. For all his lack of depth, Christian sees what the brilliant Cyrano cannot: Cyrano's words, not Christian's looks, won Roxane. Mortally wounded, Christian urges Cyrano to tell Roxane the truth. But, unable to own his success, Cyrano keeps the secret for another fourteen years. Finally, just before he dies, he reveals himself to Roxane. He may be a romantic hero, but Cyrano allows his irrational self-loathing to keep him from the life of his dreams; he misses his chance at happiness.

Irrational self-criticism isn't just an internal problem, as in Cyrano's case. I believe our outsides match our insides. In one way or another, we project our feelings, attitudes, beliefs, and opinions to others, whether we mean to or not. If you feel you're a loser, you will signal that to others. I'm sure you've been in situations where you could "read" someone else's low self-esteem despite outward signs of confidence.

When I was a banker, I met with loan applicants all the time. Most were entrepreneurs looking to borrow money to start businesses. When I first started, I was struck by the disparity between the numbers and information on the applications and in the business plan and the sense I got from sitting down and chatting with an applicant. There were times I'd get an application with excellent financials and a flawless business plan, but the applicant projected self-doubt and looming failure. Other times I'd receive a borderline application with a sketchy business plan, but the applicant gave off a confident air of guaranteed success. I told a more experienced banker about my experience, and he gave a knowing nod. He told me, "Some people have the sweet smell of success, and others just reek of failure."

There's one person who really sticks in my mind. David Powers, forty-four, had spent almost fifteen years as the chief mechanic at a high-end auto dealership just outside a major New England city. David was renowned as an expert mechanic, often being flown to Germany, where the cars were designed, to consult with engineers. When the dealership announced plans to move, David decided to open his own auto repair business. With a built-in base of affluent customers, the business seemed a natural winner. David came to the bank at which I was working and applied for a loan. When I first studied his application, everything seemed in order. David certainly had the experience, and the shop seemed a good bet to generate good revenues. But when I sat and interviewed him, the picture changed. Despite being a handsome, intelligent fellow, David appeared painfully shy. Still, I started the interview expecting it to be a mere formality. I told David I was impressed by his experience. He responded by telling me that he actually wished he'd spent less time in the shop and more out on the dealership's sales floor. I mentioned that the shop's projected numbers seemed solid. David said he hoped they'd stay that way but was afraid of what would happen if another dealership came to the area. After thirty minutes, David talked me out of the loan by repeatedly denigrating his experience and his skills.

While your own self-denigration may not be as instantly negative as David's, it will eventually affect not just your insides, but your outsides as well. Even though your negative self-assessments are irrational and just plain wrong, they will at some point chip away at your outward aura. After years of this kind of self-abuse, others will start to judge you not by what you've done, but by what you think of yourself. This applies to your personal life as well as your career or financial life.

Denise Compari, thirty-eight, is a former lingerie model who went into retail merchandising in her early thirties. It was while managing the petites department in an expensive New York City department store that the lanky blonde first met her husband, Michael Flanagan, forty-two, who is regional sales manager for a major athletic wear and equipment manufacturer. Michael played football in college, but, as he joked, his "shoulders have dropped to his belt line since then."

Denise fell instantly in love with this warm, engaging, affectionate man. But eventually, Michael's self-denigration became an issue. Whenever he got depressed, Michael made negative comments about his appearance and his lack of financial success. Denise argued with him at first, denying he was overweight and praising his career success. That didn't stop Michael from continuing to express his self-loathing. After a couple of years, Denise stopped arguing with him and instead tried to offer support. "I don't agree," she said. "But if you feel that way, I'll do whatever I can to help you do something about it." That didn't stop the negativity, either.

After four years of marriage, Denise stopped responding at all to Michael's comments. That, he said, was evidence that his self-abuse was accurate. "You didn't respond right away, so you agree I'm a loser." Denise's frustration started bubbling over. Eventually, Michael's constant drumbeat of self-damnation led Denise to, in effect, agree with him. At that point, Michael accused her of lying for years when she'd argued with him. Just before what would have been their fifth anniversary, they separated.

Denise and Michael may be an extreme case, but only in the outcome, not in the pattern. Self-denigration not only can damage your own esteem, it can easily become a self-fulfilling prophecy. Say something long enough and loud enough, and eventually, no matter how false, some people will start to agree.

It's not just in your relations with others that self-denigration will cause you harm. It can deaden your spirit and darken your soul.

Getting out from Between Your Ears

How do you stop this self-abuse and start owning your success? Cultivate humility. And how do you do that? Get out from between your ears. By looking at yourself from the outside, you can start to be realistic and feel better about yourself. You'll then project that improved self-esteem to others. Cultivate humility and you'll be able to own your success. You'll lead a happier, healthier, and more fulfilled life once you get out of your own head.

Get out from between your ears. By looking at yourself from the outside, you can start to be realistic and feel better about yourself.

Irrational self-denigration is inexorably linked to an unrealistic view of yourself. Rather than analyzing yourself based on external standards or achievements, you pronounce judgment based on internal notions of what you could have done or what you should have done. Instead of making an objective assessment, you're making a subjective assessment. For the vast majority of people, that results in a much more negative appraisal. It's as if we're suffering from a form of anorexia in which personal traits and achievements, rather than body image, are distorted. Instead of looking in the mirror and mistakenly seeing someone fat, we look in the mirror and mistakenly see someone unsuccessful and unworthy.

While digging into the reasons for your behavior may be therapeutic, I think the way to stop beating yourself up is, ironically enough, to stop thinking you're the center of the world. As the wonderful aphorist Mason Cooley once wrote, "Self-hatred and self-love are equally self-centered." By stepping outside yourself, you can begin to put yourself in a realistic context. Get out from between your ears and you can start making rational judgments.

Pattie Cultivates Humility

Pattie Townsend's journey out of the bad neighborhood between her ears began when her agent suggested Pattie join a local chapter of a national association of photographers. The idea was to find a supportive group that would turn out for shows and could provide constructive criticism. Pattie reluctantly went to a meeting of a chapter based in a city near where she lived. Of about thirty active members, two were full-time photographers. The rest all had other jobs and took photos on their off hours. When she was asked to introduce herself and talk about her work, Pattie described the trajectory of her career. Before she could start to denigrate herself, she was barraged with questions. "How did you find an agent so fast?" "You've been doing this for four years and you've had four shows already?" "You sold how many shots at your last show?" The audience, more expert at the difficulties of what Pattie had accomplished than the general public, didn't give her a chance to belittle her own accomplishments. Pattie, faced with people who hadn't achieved as much as quickly as she had, was too embarrassed to put herself down. After all, if she said she wasn't worthy, what did that say about all the people in the group? Pattie found herself in a situation where she was forced to see herself as others saw her, rather than dwelling just on how she saw herself.

Most of us don't have the kind of opportunity to be forced outside our heads that Pattie had. We can't rely on others to help us learn humility, we've got to do it on our own.

The best way to cultivate humility and get out from between your ears is to put yourself in situations where you're forced to face the fact that you're not the center of the universe. This can be done physically, spiritually, or both. The goal is to put your life in perspective. The philosopher Baruch Spinoza urged people to try to put their personal concerns and problems in the place they actually occupied in the totality of things. He believed we should look at our own lives through the eyes of eternity. If we did that, we'd see that our worries are insignificant, and that would help us bear them better.

"I Can't Teach My Daughters Self-Hatred"

Bobbie Stroud, forty-four, is a very successful college professor at a Minnesota university. A pale woman with spiky gray hair, she drives her family crazy with her self-criticism. While she's a wonderful cook, her work schedule allows her to make only one big family meal a week: Sunday dinner. She'll make an incredible meal, and when her husband, Bill, a forty-five-year-old self-employed accountant, tells her how wonderful it is, she responds by saying, "It's a little too salty," or, "The roast's a bit overdone," or with some other criticism. When her children, fourteen-year-old Enya and twelve-year-old Nicole, chime in with their compliments, Bobbie responds by saying she wishes Sunday weren't the only time she could make them this kind of meal. At the end of every semester, when Bobbie goes over her students' evaluations, she fixates on the handful of negative comments, overlooking all the praise. Bill invariably points to the multiple teaching awards hanging on her office wall, but it never seems to make a difference.

For years Bill shrugged off Bobbie's self-denigration, but that was before he began to notice the same behavior developing in both Enya and Nicole. Enya, a driven student, came home with a great report card—four A's and one B—and despite effusive praise from both Bobbie and Bill could focus only on the B as a mark of failure. Nicole, a strikingly attractive little girl, started to criticize her appearance. "My hair's too straight" and "I'm fat" became regular parts of her conversation with the rest of the family. Although aware there could be multiple reasons for the girls' self-criticism, Bill suspected that Bobbie's regular self-denigration played a role. One Saturday evening they went out for a movie, and over coffee afterward Bill expressed his concerns to Bobbie. "It's not good for you to beat yourself up all the time, and I don't think it's good for the girls, either." Bobbie almost immediately turned Bill's comments into fuel for more self-loathing. But before she could go too far down that road, Bill stopped her. "You're doing it again. You've got to stop." He then went through a litany of ways in which she was a wonderful wife, mother, and teacher.

Bill's comments and the now apparent impact on her daughters gave Bobbie pause. The momentary glimpse of herself from outside, and the awareness that her self-abuse could be damaging to her daughters, convinced Bobbie she had to do something about it. She spent a few days trying to come up with ways to start owning her successes. Bobbie decided that the best way for her to get out from between her ears was to be out alone in nature. She began by taking her canoe out on a lake near her home. Every Saturday morning she rose before dawn, paddled her canoe out to the center of the lake, and just floated. She listened to the early morning calls of the water-birds. She watched as the rays of the sun burned the fog off the lake's surface. She saw the surface of the lake come to life with ripples from fish below and insects from above. As the sun rose and lit up the trees lining the lakeshore, Bobbie felt a comforting sense of smallness. There were gaps in the trees, clouds in the sky, and rocks breaking the water's surface. She couldn't imagine a more beautiful setting, yet it wasn't perfect. In fact, it was the flaws that somehow made the setting more beautiful. They made it . . . more real. A few days after her ephiphany, she soon saw her own attitudes and behavior change. And eventually both she and Bill could see subtle changes in the girls as well.

Eager to keep her newfound perspective, Bobbie has resolved to continue her "outdoor worship sessions," as she calls them. As the weather grows colder, Bobbie plans to replace her morning canoe trips with hikes along the trail that rims the lake. She has bought snowshoes so that when winter hits she'll be able to continue her weekly communions with beautifully imperfect nature.

Bobbie's discovery of the healing power of nature is far from unique. But few have described it as eloquently as the young Anne Frank. Perhaps because she was trapped in an attic sanctuary from the Nazis and, as a result, was unable to appreciate nature up close, she could better appreciate its power: "The best remedy for those who are afraid, lonely or unhappy is to go outside, somewhere where they can be quiet, alone with the heavens, nature and God. Because only then does one feel that all is as it should be and that God wishes to see people happy, amidst the simple beauty of nature. As long as this exists, and it certainly always will, I know that there will always be comfort for every sorrow, whatever the circumstances may be. And I firmly believe that nature brings solace in all troubles."

"I'm Not Responsible for Things for Which I Wasn't Responsible"

Daniel Jackson, fifty-six, is vice president of marketing for a long established manufacturing company based on the West Coast, which recently shifted its focus from consumer to industrial products. The company's plan was to move from a fashionable but volatile market to one that, while less exciting, would offer greater stability. Daniel, a striking man with a shaved head and an omnipresent diamond earring, was recruited to the company to help it make the shift successfully. With more than thirty years of experience in the field, Daniel was seen as a vital part of the "new team." Unfortunately, things didn't go well.

The industry that the company was most counting on was telecommunications, which crashed dramatically within months of Daniel's arrival. (Since then the industry has stabilized, but it still hasn't recovered completely.) Daniel did all he could. He created solid relationships with a whole new group of customers. The company, despite joining the industry only recently, became a recognized leader in the business. Daniel's input in new product development helped put the company in position to take advantage of an industry turnaround. The firm's market share now actually exceeds projections—it's just that the market has shrunk in size. But that hasn't stopped Daniel from beating himself up.

For months, upper management went out of its way to praise Daniel's efforts. Every time he finished his reports by offering an apology for not doing even more, or for not turning the business around single-handedly, the upper management team corrected him, saying he and his staff were doing a great job, reiterating that no one was faulting Daniel and that the company thought he was doing a great job playing the poor hand he had been dealt. But Daniel's almost reflexive self-criticism started to have an effect. Over time, the corrections from management weren't as quick, nor did they seem to be as heartfelt.

This was noticed by Daniel's closest associate, the vice president of advertising and public relations. One evening over drinks after work, he suggested Daniel stop providing ammunition to the upper management team. "There's scuttlebutt the board is now looking for some scalps," he revealed. "There are a couple of guys in the management group who were responsible for this new strategy but who'd be happy to offer up your head as a sacrifice to save their own."

Daniel knew his friend was right. To keep from digging his own grave, he realized he'd need to stop viewing himself as the company's potential savior. He had to evaluate his performance based not on what he thought he should accomplish, but on what he actually was accomplishing, which was a great deal. Daniel decided he needed to cultivate humility.

Every day on his drive to the office, Daniel passed a sign indicating the road to a Catholic monastery. Since he was a compulsive early riser and was routinely at his desk by 7:30, Daniel figured he had time to stop off one morning and visit the monastery. At about 6:30 a.m., he pulled off the main highway and turned onto a gravel road that climbed up a heavily wooded hill. Near the top of the hill, the scenery opened up to a pastoral vista of fields, meadows, and barns. Standing out among the rustic buildings was a simple, modern chapel. Daniel parked his car and entered the open door. Inside was a spartan, airy, wood-accented sanctuary lit entirely by candles. As if on cue, Daniel heard chanting and footsteps. As he took a seat on a wooden bench near the chapel door, he saw a file of monks begin to emerge from a lower floor. Wearing simple brown robes over blue jeans and work boots, the monks filled two benches on either side of the stone altar. They sat facing one another and chanted prayers for approximately ten minutes. Then they rose and walked back downstairs.

As he left the chapel, Daniel saw the monks emerge from another door. Three monks went over to a nearby barn, another to a tractor parked alongside the chapel; others headed up a path to other barns and outbuildings. As Daniel walked back to his car, he realized that, like the monks, he was heading out to do his daily work. He also realized he was going to work with a renewed sense of the infinite. Daniel was suddenly struck by how this simple act of morning devotion could help him keep things in perspective.

Since his first discovery of the monastery, Daniel has been able largely to overcome his self-denigration at work. He is assembling material for his next review, at which he plans to ask for a salary increase. And he's still stopping off at the monastery every morning before work.

"I Can't Help Everyone"

Tom Corrocan, thirty-four, an angular man with short, straight blond hair, is a social worker for a charitable agency that helps impoverished families in New York City. His friends and family call Tom an idealist. Although he had the grades to go on to law school, Tom chose to get a master's degree in social work instead so he'd be able to have a greater positive impact on people's lives. For years, Tom worked for a program that helped the long-term unemployed gain new skills and find work. But after September 11 his focus, and that of his agency, changed.

Tom's office is less than two miles from the World Trade Center. He was at his desk when the first plane struck. He heard about it from his partner, Jack, who saw the initial impact on the tower from a park across the river. Tom and his co-workers ran to the window and, through the smoke, saw the second plane hit. The rest of the day became a blur—the crowds walking uptown, the dazed faces of people on the ferry crossing the river, the frantic calls on his cell phone from family and friends across the country. At some point, Tom realized his life and his work would never be the same.

Like most of New York City's social service organizations, Tom's agency joined the effort to help those affected by the attacks. Because of his experience working with the unemployed, Tom joined a project to help many of the lower-income service workers whose jobs vanished along with the towers. Despite the poor job market, Tom blamed himself for his inability to find all his clients jobs. He could feel he was losing his sense of optimism and enthusiasm and needed to turn his attitude around.

A nationally ranked cross-country runner in college, Tom hadn't done much running since coming to New York. But he remembered the high he got from running, a feeling that he was part of the larger world. Tom decided to take up running again.

Every day after work, Tom changed into running clothes, put his work clothes and briefcase in a locker, and headed up to Central Park. Once he entered the park, the sounds of the city started to grow quiet. After a number of laps, the self-deprecating voice in his head also started to grow quiet, replaced by the sound of his shoes hitting the pavement and the wind rustling through the trees. After a few months of running, Tom could sense his attitude changing. His old optimism was returning. He was focusing on what was going right rather than what was going wrong. He was beginning to own his success.

Whether it's spending time in nature, or prayer, or exercise, the result is the same. I know people who take up stargazing. Others become gardeners. That would make sense to Thornton Wilder, who once wrote, "The planting of trees is the least self-centered of all that we do." However you do it, by taking time to see how you fit in the world, you gain perspective; you cultivate a sense of humility and get out from between your ears; and you learn to own your success.

The reason all these efforts at finding perspective work is that they are, in one way or another, acts of surrender. "The way to success as vouched by innumerable authentic personal narratives is . . . by . . . surrender . . . ," wrote William James. He urged readers to "give up the feeling of responsibility, let go your hold, resign the care of your destiny to higher powers."

It's ironic, but through surrender self-esteem rises. Stop viewing yourself as the center of the universe and you'll be able to accept your own shortcomings and failings. That will enable you to own your successes. But just as welcome as the boost to self-esteem is the realization of your place in the world. According to Henry David Thoreau, "Humility, like darkness, reveals the heavenly lights." However you define the higher power in the universe, surrendering will bring you closer to it.

Own Your Success

- We do things to ourselves we'd never let others get away with and think things about ourselves we'd never let others say without challenge.

- This isn't criticism designed for self-improvement, it's denigration designed to beat ourselves up for not meeting our own impossible standards.
- We need to own our success as well as our failures in order to live life to the fullest and be happy.
- To do that, we need to get out from between our ears and see ourselves realistically. We need to cultivate an attitude of humility.
- That comes by surrendering, placing ourselves in situations where we're clearly not the center of the universe. Through surrender we increase self-esteem.

(5)

YOU DON'T HAVE TO GO IT ALONE

Ask, and it shall be given you; seek, and ye shall
find; knock, and it shall be opened unto you.
—*Matthew 7:7*

Are there times you feel powerless? Well, your reach and strength could be limitless. You can double your borrowing power. You can triple the size of your professional network. You can geometrically multiply your odds of finding a mate or making friends. You can acquire the wisdom and expertise it normally takes years, and maybe tens of thousands of dollars, to learn. And all this can be done quickly and easily. Just ask for help. Getting help is the easiest way for you to leverage your time, money, skill, and knowledge. Help can lead to happiness.

Yet most of us hesitate to reach out. We don't ask to borrow money from a sister to help pay for our daughter's medical bill. We refuse to ask our co-worker for job leads. We're too proud to ask our cousin if she knows any single women. We hesitate to show we know less about hanging shelves than our brother-in-law. We routinely pass up opportunities to make our lives easier and more satisfying simply because we don't ask for help. Well, it's time for this to stop.

We routinely pass up opportunities to make our lives easier and more satisfying simply because we don't ask for help.

You don't have to go it alone. You don't have to be Superman or Wonder Woman. You can reach out to others and, in the process, get their help in creating the life of your dreams. In fact, I believe you need to reach out to others to live life to the fullest. The psychologist O. Hobart Mowrer once wrote, "You alone can do it, but you cannot do it alone." "Nothing we do, however virtuous," wrote the theologian Reinhold Niebuhr, "can be accomplished alone; therefore we are saved by love."

I don't think Mowrer and Niebuhr had Frodo Baggins in mind when they wrote those lines, but the Hobbit hero of J. R. R. Tolkien's *The Lord of the Rings* is a perfect example of someone trying do something noble who can't do it alone, who is, in the end, saved by love. Frodo takes on the burden of bringing the one ring of power back to the mountain where it was forged and destroying it. The problem is that the mountain lies deep in the land of Mordor, controlled by Sauron, the evil Dark Lord. Frodo, feeling the burden is his alone and not wishing to endanger anyone else, starts off on his own. But his friend Sam refuses to abandon him and, reluctantly, Frodo accepts his help. Later on, Frodo decides to enlist the evil creature Gollum to guide him and Sam. Sam offers help to Frodo out of love, and Frodo refuses to kill Gollum out of pity. In the end, Frodo needs both Sam and Gollum to complete his quest. It's only by receiving help that Frodo succeeds.

I don't think he's ever before been compared to Frodo Baggins, but Michael Jordan also needed the help of others to succeed. Despite being the greatest player in the history of basketball, Jordan couldn't single-handedly lead his Chicago Bulls to a world championship. It was only after two other extraordinary players, Scottie Pippen and Dennis Rodman, joined Jordan that the Bulls became champions. If Michael Jordan admitted he needed help, don't you think you can as well?

I know: you're probably still hesitant. People seem reflexively to shy away from asking for assistance. There's a Chinese proverb: "It's easier to go up into the mountains to catch tigers than to ask others for help." Indeed, whenever I first suggest to clients that they ask for help, they look as if I've advised them to go catch a tiger. When I ask why they're hesitant, they say something like "I should be able to do this on my own." Then they'll add a caveat along the lines of "And no one would help me anyway." Both reasons are utter nonsense. The first excuse is a misreading of history. The second rationalization shows a misunderstanding of human nature.

"I Shouldn't Need Help to Lose Weight"

Keith Affa, forty-six, has been struggling with his weight ever since college. A big guy even when young, he had kept in good shape by playing football and baseball. Later, when in his thirties, Keith went on crash diets of his own design whenever he felt his jeans getting tight. After he married Lisa, however, he stopped paying as much attention. His job as regional sales manager for a computer software company had Keith on the road most of the week. That meant meals grabbed on the road or in airports, lots of customer dinners, and hour after hour spent on the telephone, behind the wheel of his car, or in an airplane seat.

Lisa also put on weight after they first married. Having two children in five years didn't help. But once both girls were in school all day, the curvy blonde was able to find the time to go to aerobics classes and Weight Watchers meetings. She changed to a healthier cooking style at home and suggested Keith go on walks with her when he was home; but neither helped Keith to lose weight.

Three years ago, impressed with the results Lisa was getting, Keith announced his New Year's resolution to drop fifty pounds. That has been his resolution ever since. First he went on the Ornish diet and started playing golf. He stuck with that diet for two months and lost ten pounds, but gradually he put it all back on. His golf habit lasted longer, but soon he was riding in carts rather than carrying his clubs. Next he tried Atkins. He stuck with that longer, dropping twenty pounds and feeling fit enough to carry his golf bag again. But after six months he started slipping off the wagon, then gained back the weight. That led him to the South Beach diet, which he was convinced would do the trick. He announced his decision to Lisa on New Year's, as he had twice before. This time, she snapped.

"You have to take better care of yourself," she pleaded. "It's not just the two of us anymore. We've got the girls to think of."

Keith knew she was right. He promised he'd finally lose the weight and told her what he'd just read about South Beach. Before he could go into the details, however, Lisa cut him off.

"I want you to go talk to someone—a nutritionist, a doctor, or a therapist. You need help."

Keith's anger flared and he snapped back, "I shouldn't need help to lose weight."

The Myth of Rugged Individualism

Like most of us, Keith had been taught that individuals could succeed on their own. History books tell us our nation has been shaped by brave pioneers who overcame the dangers of the frontier relying solely on the strength of their individual characters and abilities. From the homesteader taming the wilderness to the solo entrepreneur creating an industry, our culture lionizes self-made soloists. Growing up, we're given effusive praise whenever we do something on our own: "Junior drew that picture all by himself!" We hear universal admiration for individuals who make something of themselves unaided: "He worked as a janitor and put himself through medical school." As a result, we're conditioned to believe we need to succeed on our own; that asking for help is a sign of weakness or admission of failure.

Although the inclination here may be to blame our parents, or the founding fathers, I think the fault lies with a history professor named Frederick Jackson Turner. In 1893, he presented a paper titled "The Significance of the Frontier in American History" at an academic conference in Chicago. Turner's paper suggests the American character is unique and comes not from European influences, but from the presence of a great frontier—the border between "savagery and civilization." The paper portrays those who settled the wilderness as the embodiments of the qualities that make America great. At the time of the conference, social Darwinism was in vogue, there were increased tensions between eastern and western states, and that most individualist of presidents, Teddy Roosevelt, was creating an American empire. In 1928, Republican presidential candidate Herbert Hoover gave the set of qualities a catchy name— "rugged individualism"—and successfully used it as a way to differentiate his own beliefs from those of his Democratic opponent, Governor Al Smith.

After that, the notion of rugged individualism as an essential character trait became entrenched, impacting everything from politics to family lives. "Our treatment of both older people and children," wrote anthropologist Margaret Mead, "reflects the value we place on independence and autonomy. We do our best to make our children independent from birth. We leave them all alone in rooms with the lights out and tell them, 'Go to sleep by yourselves.' And the old people we respect most are the ones who will fight for their independence, who would sooner starve to death than ask for help."

The problem with this attitude is that it's wrong. It's based on a skewed reading of history. When it comes to defining the key to America's success, you can make a stronger case for people helping one another than you can for rugged individualism. The founding fathers relied not only on the help of the founding mothers, but on the strong backs of their slaves. The government purchased most of the western lands and sent the army west to clear it of the native population. Pioneers joined together into wagon trains so they could pool their efforts and maximize the chances of success. Settlements were built by communities, neighbors constructing one another's homes and raising one another's barns. It was the railroad that spread civilization throughout the West.

Fast-forward in history and you can look behind most of what we think of as great individual feats and find a group effort. Henry David Thoreau was visited at Walden Pond by ladies from town who provided him with home-baked pies and, odds are, other, more personal treats. Thomas Edison had a staff of scientists and engineers working with him in his New Jersey lab. Charles Lindbergh may have flown alone, but his plane was designed and built by the staff of the Ryan Aircraft Company in St. Louis. Bill Gates worked with college pal Paul Allen in founding Microsoft, and Steve Jobs had Steve Wozniak with him in the garage that spawned Apple Computer. Even Gary Cooper needed the help of Grace Kelly to win the gunfight in *High Noon.*[*]

I think psychologist and human development specialist Urie

---

[*]Directed by Fred Zinnemann and written by John W. Cunningham and Carl Foreman.

Bronfenbrenner said it best: "Witness the American ideal: the Self-Made Man. But there is no such person. If we can stand on our own two feet, it is because others have raised us up. If, as adults, we can lay claim to competence and compassion, it only means that other human beings have been willing and enabled to commit their competence and compassion to us—through infancy, childhood, and adolescence, right up to this very moment."

> If we can stand on our own two feet, it is because others have raised us up. If, as adults, we can lay claim to competence and compassion, it only means that other human beings have been willing and enabled to commit their competence and compassion to us—through infancy, childhood, and adolescence, right up to this very moment.
> —Urie Bronfenbrenner

These two competing threads—self-reliance and community— weave their way through American culture. Our art, our values, our political parties, even our heroes, can be seen as representing one or the other thread at different times. Finding a balance between the two is part of the challenge we face as Americans.

"No One Is Going to Help Me with a Business Plan"

Tori Scudder, thirty, never dreamed she'd become a pastry chef. It was always assumed that the zaftig, vibrant woman, daughter of two college professor parents, would become some kind of professional. After three years at the same university where both her parents teach, Tori felt the need to escape. When the opportunity came to study in Vienna for her final semester, she grabbed it. She fell in love with the city's café culture, particularly its extraordinary cakes and pastries. After returning home, she had barely finished unpacking when her parents asked about graduate school. Feeling pressured, Tori opted to pursue a master's degree in French history.

While taking an advanced French language class, she met Henrietta Levine. A local restaurateur, Henrietta was taking the French class to prepare for an extended trip to Paris to study baking at a culinary school. Henrietta's restaurant specialized in continental fare and was very successful. But at the time, she felt her desserts were lacking. She decided it would be easier to train herself for the job than to find a pastry chef. One day after class, Tori told Henrietta of her love of Vienna's cafés. After hearing Tori wax poetic over napoleons and éclairs, Henrietta commented that Tori should be the one to go to Paris and become a baker. Tori laughed about it at the time but spent the rest of the day and night daydreaming. Unable to sleep that night, she contemplated what she wanted to do with the rest of her life. By the next morning, she had decided to go to Paris to learn to be a pastry chef. Eight months later, Tori arrived back home to assume the job as Henrietta's pastry chef.

Tori worked happily at the restaurant for six years. But as time passed, she began to feel constrained. She wanted to expand her offerings and try new things, but Henrietta didn't want to shake up the menu too much. While going over her taxes with her accountant, Tori admitted to feeling stifled. "Why don't you open your own shop," her accountant suggested. "You're well-known, and I think I can come up with a number of people who might be willing to invest if you have a good business plan."

"I don't have any experience in running a business," Tori responded reflexively.

"But you know every restaurateur in this town," her accountant objected. "I'm sure you can go to some of them for advice."

Tori shook her head: "No one is going to help me with a business plan."

The Myth of Indifference

Tori's not the only one who thinks no one would be willing to
help her. When I am dispelling people of the need to tackle obstacles alone in order to be truly successful, I'm often hit with
backup arguments that echo Tori's fear: "No one will help me
anyway." I don't know if such cynicism or fear of rejection is a
recent phenomenon. What I do know is that it's wrong.

One of the most powerful sentences in the English language
is "I have a problem and I need your help." That's because men-
tally healthy human beings are innately helpful. When push
comes to shove, and one human being asks another for help,
race, religion, national origin, age, gender, sexual orientation,
or physical ability doesn't matter. Faced with another human in
need, we always respond as best we can.

Every longtime big-city dweller learns to create personal barriers to block out the constant assault on the senses that comes
from having so many people so close together. One of those de-
fenses is ignoring casual appeals from strangers. Just try asking
fellow pedestrians in a busy city for the time and you'll experience the phenomenon firsthand. It's a natural reaction to a lifetime of dealing constantly with panhandlers and proselytizers.
But this defense is as shallow as it is widespread. When someone is truly in need, even city dwellers respond—witness September 11, 2001. We're all familiar with the stories of the
selfless heroism of New York's firefighters and police. But hidden in the shadows of those incredible tales of heroism are

thousands, perhaps millions, of lesser acts of selflessness: the passerby who lent a distraught stranger a cell phone to make a call; the store owner who passed out water and food without thought of payment; the file clerk who sheltered a co-worker in her home; the cab driver who turned off his meter and filled his car with people who needed rides.

Sadly, that day is also a reminder that human beings can commit heinous crimes. People are capable of killing innocents, even committing genocide. But such horrors happen only when the perpetrators are taught to view their victims as less than human. They are the exceptions that prove the rule. God has programmed us to be our brother's keeper. Cain was an aberration, not a model for humanity. We're descended from Seth, who was neither murderer nor victim.

God has programmed us to be our brother's keeper. Cain was an aberration, not a model for humanity. We're descended from Seth, who was neither murderer nor victim.

God's programming is so powerful, it can be changed only through prolonged brainwashing and the twisting of His message. If you ask for help, people will respond. Sure, if you're stuck on the side of the road with a flat tire on a snowy night, some cars will pass by. But I honestly believe most people driving by will think, There but for the grace of God go I, or, I'd want someone to stop and help my daughter, and they will stop and help if they can. Those who don't will feel guilt.

Not only will people respond when asked for help, many times they'll be flattered by the request. A request for help can be an admission that the other person has something you lack or an indication of your admiration. Ask your father to help you change the oil in your car and you're saying to him: "You know more about cars than I do, Dad." He'll be glad to help since it's an ego boost for him. Ask your mother for help in making Christmas dinner and you're saying to her: "Mom, I respect your skill as a cook and a hostess." She'll gladly pitch in since it makes her feel good. I wouldn't go so far as to say you're doing Uncle Jim a favor by asking him for a $5,000 loan, but you are admitting that he has more money than you and that he's more financially savvy. Those may not be sufficient reasons for him to forgo interest, but they could be sufficient kudos for him to make the loan.

How to Ask for Help

Don't feel bad analyzing other people in this way. Understanding the needs and wants of the person you're asking for help is essential. You're not trying to manipulate the other party; you're trying to create an environment conducive to his or her natural willingness to help. I truly believe people want to help. The reason some people may hesitate, or refuse, is that something could be standing in the way of their natural inclination. Let's say you're back stranded on the road with a flat tire. One person may drive by because he's late for an appointment and thinks helping will take too much time. Another person may drive by because she's alone and is afraid of stopping for a stranger. Both deep down would like to help, but there are things standing in their way. The same is true of someone you ask for help in finding a job, for a loan to buy a car, or to watch your children for an evening. There may be obstacles, real or imagined, that could keep them from giving you the help they'd like. It's up to you to overcome those obstacles, or at least minimize them to the extent possible. For instance, while you may not be able to overcome the time constraints facing the first driver who passes by, you could minimize the fears of the second driver by having your children visible outside the car so you appear more like Bill Cosby than Ted Bundy. I've discovered there are three steps you can take to make it easier for people to say yes.

The first thing to do to make it easier for people to help is to think about what obstacles they might face. Let's say you need to ask your friend to baby-sit for your daughter on Friday night so you can visit your mother in the hospital. Your friend may already have plans for Friday night, or she may not be comfortable entertaining a small child. Having thought about the possible obstacles, you next need to think of ways they could be overcome. For example, you could be flexible enough to change your visitation schedule to match your friend's social calendar, or you could make sure to lay in a supply of new DVDs, or you could leave only after your daughter has gone to bed. The idea is to preempt possible obstacles or objections, clearing the way for the other person's natural desire to help.

The second thing you can do to make it easier for people to help is to explain your request. Why are you approaching this person for help? My guess is it's because there's something that uniquely qualifies him as the best candidate; it could be he knows more about a subject than anyone else you know. That would be the case if you were approaching your brother-in-law the carpenter for help in hanging those pesky shelves. Or perhaps she has more experience in doing something than you. For instance, you could be asking your co-worker for advice in dealing with a tough client a month after she closed a big deal with a similarly difficult customer. The key is to be able to express the reason for singling out this person. Not only will that make the person feel special, but it will reinforce his or her positive feelings for you.

The third step in making it easier for someone to help is to frame it as a specific request for help "with a problem." I've already written about the magic of saying, "I have a problem and I need your help." Asking for help automatically humbles you. Adding that you have a problem amplifies this effect without turning you into a supplicant. You're humbly asking for someone to aid your own efforts; you're not begging for someone to replace you or take over your responsibility. Making your request very specific demonstrates this is a short-term, probably onetime appeal: this isn't going to require an ongoing commitment from the other party. Let's go back to the situation of asking someone to watch your daughter while you visit your mother in the hospital. Asking for your friend's help for this one evening when, perhaps, your husband can't cover for you makes it far easier for her to accept than if you made a general, out-of-context request for help. To which of these two requests would you be more likely to say yes:

- "My mother's in the hospital and I need to visit her. Could you watch my daughter on Friday night?"
- "I have a problem and I need your help. I need to visit my mother in the hospital one evening this week, but Frank is out of town on business. Little Frannie is more comfortable with you than any of our other friends. Is there some night this week when you think you could watch her for a couple of hours?"

I know it may at first seem unnatural to go through this kind of conscious process when asking for help. But I think that's only because we're so uncomfortable even asking. When you think about it, this is the kind of mental process we go through almost reflexively for all sorts of other planned interactions. In business, when you're about to call a client or speak with a vendor, you organize your thoughts and language without giving it a moment's thought. When you're ordering a meal in a restaurant, you come up with a list of your wants and needs and present them in an organized manner. And when you ask someone out on a date, you phrase it in the way most likely to get a yes. The more often you consciously go through this three-step process of asking for help, the more ingrained it will become. Eventually you'll do it without thinking, and it will become the most natural thing in the world.

Getting Used to Asking for Help

To get to that stage, however, you'll need to become accustomed to asking for help. That's okay, since I think it's important for you to practice. After a lifetime of being taught you should do things on your own, the best way to force yourself to realize it's okay to ask for help is to enter into a concerted help campaign. From now on, frame all your requests for assistance, no matter how large or small, as requests for help. Need your friend to pick you up at the auto dealership because you're dropping off the car for a tune-up? Ask for his help with a problem: "Jon, I have a problem and need your help. Can you give me a ride home from the auto dealer tomorrow afternoon?" Have to telephone your sister and ask for her chestnut stuffing recipe? Ask for her help with a problem. "Mindy, I have a problem and need your help. Could you give me your chestnut stuffing recipe?" Find yourself slicing all your drives? Ask for help with a problem. "Mike, I have a problem and need your help. Could you watch my swing and give me some advice on what to do to keep from slicing my drives?"

I'm not suggesting you consciously go through the three-step process I outlined earlier every time you ask your spouse to pass the remote control. But I am urging you to use the language of asking for help as often as makes sense throughout the course of your normal life. That way, the idea that asking for help is a sign of weakness will gradually disappear. The more you "ask for help" and then receive it, without either feeling like, or being treated as, a failure, the sooner you'll internalize that it's not a big deal to ask for help. And the more often you consciously go through the three-step process, the sooner it will become second nature.

Help Others Whenever You Can

I don't know if it directly helps you get used to asking for help, but I think it's important you help others whenever you can. If you think you can be of assistance to someone, offer to help without waiting to be asked. Don't calculate if there's a possible quid pro quo—whether this person could be of assistance to you in the future. That's not the point. This individual may be in a position to help you in the future, or he or she may not. That doesn't matter. What counts is that you're assisting someone who needs it. I honestly believe such efforts will pay dividends for you in the future. I don't know that I'd call it justice or karma. All I know is the more you help others, the more others will help you. I've given up trying to explain it. I just accept it.

"What's the Best Way to Approach Single Women at Work?"

Asking for help is anything but second nature for Paul Richards. Paul's friends nicknamed the thirty-four-year-old attorney "Control King" years ago. A bookish-looking, slight man, Paul shrugs off the jokes about his neuroses. He feels his attention to detail and preparation are two of the keys to his having graduated college and law school with honors and to his being one of the youngest associates ever to have made partner at the prestigious firm where he works. Paul hates to rely on anyone else, whether it has to do with his work or his personal life. But as his thirty-fifth birthday nears, he's starting to question his approach.

Paul is the last of his group of friends to remain single. He dated a bit in college but was focused primarily on his studies. The same was true for law school. And then when he landed his job with the firm, he had even less time for a social life. Deep down, however, Paul knows his studies and workload also provided a comfortable rationalization for his lack of a social life. Truth be told, he's uncomfortable in social settings and, as a result, avoids the kind of parties and clubs where most of his friends have met their spouses. That leaves work as the only place to meet someone. There are a couple of single women at the firm who Paul thinks are interesting. But he's afraid that asking support staff out on dates will be seen as inappropriate if it isn't done smoothly. And he's anything but smooth.

Paul didn't want to "seem like a loser" by asking his friends for advice. But when his friends suggested taking him out to dinner for his birthday, and he realized he'd be the only single person there, Paul knew he had to do something. He decided to ask his friend Tim Leonard for help. Tim, thirty-five, an advertising space salesman for a photography magazine, was married with two young children and able to stand out in any social setting.

Paul first analyzed what obstacles Tim might have to helping. Tim might not actually know any single women, or he might not feel comfortable setting Paul up with any he did know. He decided that instead of asking Tim if he knew any eligible women, he'd ask him for general advice on how best to approach women, particularly the women at work. He'd explain that he was asking Tim because of his unequaled skill at being able to connect with strangers. Finally, he thought he'd make the request specifically about how best to ask a woman at the office to his birthday party.

The next night over a beer after work, Paul turned to his friend and said, "Tim, I have a problem and I need your help. I've never seen anyone as good at connecting with other people as you, so I'd love some advice. I want to ask a woman at the office to come with me to my birthday dinner, but I'm afraid it will seem like harassment. What's the best way to approach single women at work?"

"Would You Mind Taking a Look at My Résumé?"

Penny Linderman, forty-three, a statuesque woman who could be a body double for Lucy Lawless, has never had a problem with social interaction. Her problem is that she's having a hard time getting a new job. After ten years as the manager of the gift department in an upscale department store, she feels she's gone as far as possible in this industry. Of course, she's felt that way for the past three years, during which time she's applied for a number of other jobs without getting many bites. The problem is that she's afraid of asking for help. Since she graduated college, she's prided herself on being able to get by on her own. Her mother was widowed at an early age and instilled in Penny the importance of being able to take care of herself. Penny has traveled extensively, taken courses at various colleges, dated quite a bit, and even bought a home of her own—a lovely condominium. She feels she should be able to get a job on her own as well. After all, it's not rocket science, it's job hunting.

Despite that, she's had little luck in her search so far. She occasionally gets a call from a human resources department for further information, and she's gone on a couple of interviews for jobs for which she is overqualified. But all things considered, her efforts have been unsuccessful.

The last straw came when Penny answered an ad that could have been written specifically for her. Despite obviously fitting the requirements to a tee, she didn't get a call back. That convinced her she needed help. But she didn't know where to turn. As an only child, Penny had no siblings to turn to for help. Of her close friends, two were stay-at-home moms who hadn't been in the job market for years and the third was a schoolteacher who had been at the same junior high school for more than twenty years. Penny worried that if she approached any of her vendor contacts, they'd leak word to her employer that she was looking for another job. There was one possibility: a new manager, Melissa, who had come to the store after stints in public relations, advertising, and television production. Penny decided to ask Melissa for help.

Penny knew there would be obstacles to Melissa's helping her out. Since she and Melissa were peers, they could conceivably be competing for the same jobs in the future. In addition, it was possible Melissa might let word slip that Penny was looking for another job. Despite those potential problems, Penny thought Melissa was the best person to ask since she'd obviously been able to change careers repeatedly. While she wouldn't have minded some general career-changing advice, Penny decided to narrow her request.

Early one morning, Penny waited outside the store for Melissa to arrive. When she did, Penny made her pitch: "Melissa, I have a problem and need your help. I've never met anyone who has been able to move from one industry to another as well as you have. I've been investigating ways to shift industries, but I don't think I've got a handle on things. I'd love to get your advice. Would you mind taking a look at my résumé?"

"Could You Give Me My Inheritance Early?"

Ken Walker, fifty-one, has finally found the perfect business. The problem is that he doesn't have enough money to buy it.

For years, Ken, a stocky man with closely cropped gray hair, searched for the right opportunity. Although he made a good living working in the finance department of a major insurance company, he never really enjoyed his job. But while his kids were growing up and his wife, Patricia, was getting her postgraduate degrees, he needed the security it offered. Still, he spent hours each weekend reading about franchise opportunities and looking through newspapers and trade magazines for businesses that were up for sale. Two years ago, Patricia landed a job as a full-time professor at a local college. Suddenly the couple's income doubled, and one of their financial obligations shrank: a benefit of Patricia's employment was drastically reduced tuition for the children of faculty. Suddenly freed of the need for providing financial stability, Ken redoubled his efforts to find a business.

One day, while looking through the business section of his local newspaper, he saw an article about a local entrepreneur who was looking to retire. The entrepreneur ran a fleet of four food trucks that provided everything from breakfasts, hot and cold subs, pizzas, and soft drinks to over-the-counter medications and condoms. The trucks were fixtures on the campuses of the four colleges in the area, drawing customers primarily from the student dorms. Although the physical assets of the business weren't that sizable—just the four trucks and the contents of a small rented warehouse—the goodwill and entrenched customer base were incredible. The trucks were informal local landmarks and were the only such operations with the right to operate on each campus.

Ken arranged a meeting with the owner, and the two hit it off right away. The books showed the trucks were, in Ken's words to Patricia, "a license to print money." The hours would be long since he'd be running one truck, and he'd need to hold on to the three other drivers, but it was just the kind of small, hands-on, customer-oriented business for which he had been searching. After meeting with his attorney and accountant, and having some informal negotiations with the owner and his team of professionals, Ken came up with an estimate of how much he needed to buy the business. Using their savings and tapping into their home equity would leave Ken $20,000 short.

Ken had put himself through college by working nights. He and Patricia had lived frugally to maintain their independence. Through the years, they'd been able to stand on their own, taking out a mortgage to buy their home and student loans for Patricia's education. While he wasn't happy about it, Ken realized he'd need to get help if he was going to be able to buy the business.

He sat down one evening to go over all the people he knew who might be able to provide the needed money. One friend of his was a successful attorney who might be willing to loan him the money, but Ken didn't want to go further into debt if he could avoid it. While discussing the options, Ken's attorney casually asked if he had any accounts receivable in his personal life, such as an anticipated inheritance. It was then that Ken remembered his father had set aside $25,000 for him in his will, a sum his mother had maintained in a separate account for the past ten years. After discussing it with Patricia, Ken decided he'd ask his mother for his inheritance early.

Ken knew financial need might be a perceived, if not actual, issue for his mother. His father's pension and Social Security and his parents' savings provided his mother with a sufficient income. Still, she might look on the $25,000 as part of her safety net. He also believed the idea of an early inheritance might be a bit too untraditional for her to be comfortable with right away. He decided to approach his mother for the simple reason that she was the only person he knew who could provide him with the money. She was also, other than Patricia, the one person who most wanted to see him happy. Finally, he knew he needed to make it clear to his mother that he needed the money to buy this specific business and that it could be structured as a short-term loan if necessary.

While all this was more than he could convey in just a few sentences, Ken broached the subject after dinner at his mother's house: "Mom, I have a problem and I need your help. I know that, more than anything else, you want me to be happy. I've finally found the business I've been looking for, but the only way I can buy it is to, at least temporarily, tap into the money Dad left for me. Could you give me my inheritance early?"

Forget all the notions of rugged individualism you've been taught over the years. And give up all those fears and doubts that others would be willing to help you. Asking for help, in matters large and small, can make all the difference in your life. You'll be able to afford things you otherwise couldn't. You'll be able to achieve goals in your career you thought were out of reach. And you'll be able to lead a richer and more satisfying personal life. Don't let pride or cynicism stand in the way of your improving your life. Your opportunities are unlimited if you're willing to ask for help.

Don't let pride or cynicism stand in the way of your improving your life.

You Don't Have to Go It Alone

- Getting help is the easiest way for you to leverage your time, money, and knowledge.
- People think they should be able to do things on their own or that others won't help them.
- Both rationalizations are wrong. Rugged individualism is a myth, and God has programmed people to be helpful.
- Make it easier for people to help you by offering ways to overcome their obstacles, explaining why you're approaching them, and framing your request as help for a specific problem.
- Practice asking for help as much as you can, and help others whenever you can.

(6)

THERE'S NO TIME LIKE NOW, SO TAKE THE ACTION

Never stop because you're afraid—you are never so likely to be wrong.

—*Fridtjof Nansen*

D
o you ever find yourself waiting for the perfect moment to make a dreaded telephone call or to tackle a problem assignment? Waiting for the perfect moment means waiting forever. Hesitation delays success, not pain, and freezes fear in place. Be dauntless. Take the action. You'll achieve more, be happier, and spend less time worried and afraid.

Waiting for the perfect moment means waiting forever. Hesitation delays success, not pain, and freezes fear in place.

There are times when all of us have trouble taking an action. We plan, prepare, and plot a course, but when the moment comes, we hesitate. Sometimes it's in minor matters of little long-term impact, like deciding whether or not to buy a suit that's on sale or choosing what to order at a restaurant. Other times it's in major issues, such as whether or not to make an offer on a particular house that's for sale or when and how to tell a spouse you want a divorce. Some of us make a habit of delay, and it becomes procrastination—an ingrained character flaw. Others fall victim in just one area of life—say, dealings with employees—or in just a handful of situations a year. Occasionally, hesitancy renders the question moot: a teen learns the girl he has delayed asking to the prom has agreed to go with someone else, or the job candidate a business owner was thinking of hiring accepts an offer elsewhere. Most often, though, the delay prolongs pain, anxiety, or discomfort.

That was certainly the effect on Stevens, the butler whose story serves as the basis of Kazuo Ishiguro's wonderful novel *The Remains of the Day*. Stevens seems cold, snobbish, and almost entirely without humor. He says he's devoted to a life of selfless dedication and service to the lord of the house. He takes a strange pride in responding impassively to his own father's death. Stevens squabbles tirelessly with the head housekeeper, Miss Kenton, about what is right and proper. But as the book progresses, it's clear that Stevens is deceiving himself. In perhaps its saddest subplot, Stevens denies and delays ever speaking with Miss Kenton about their obvious mutual attraction. Years go by, with Stevens always having some excuse to create or maintain distance from Miss Kenton. Finally she leaves the house. Years later, when there's an opening for a new housekeeper, Stevens seeks out Miss Kenton. Although superficially he's meeting her about the job, it's obvious he's also exploring the possibility of their finally getting together. It turns out that she married soon after leaving her job at the house. While the marriage was unhappy and is now over, she explains to Stevens that it's too late for her to come back to work at the house and, the subtext is clear, it's also too late for them to get together romantically. The book ends with Stevens realizing too late that he has wasted his life. His delay and denial lost him a chance at happiness.

Whatever the reason for Stevens's hesitancy, it's clear delay ruins his life. The same could be true for your own hesitation. Even if the effect isn't as dramatic, hesitation will certainly never improve your situation. Most often it makes things worse. So why do we do it? The answer's simple: fear.

There are times we hesitate taking an action because we're afraid of failure. You don't ask your attractive co-worker out for coffee because you're worried he'll reject you. You don't ask your supervisor for a salary increase because you're frightened she'll turn you down. Other times we hesitate because we're not sure what will happen and we're afraid of the unknown. You delay going to a new church because you're not sure the congregation will be welcoming. You hold off visiting a potential customer because you don't know if she'll be cordial.

Kira Howard, forty-seven, kept putting off a visit to her ailing childhood friend, Miranda Washington. The two women had been very close throughout their thirties when both were single and living in the downtown area of a city in the Northwest. But when Kira married and moved out to the suburbs, she and Miranda began drifting apart. There was no dramatic split, but time passed. By the time Kira learned Miranda had been diagnosed with amyotrophic lateral sclerosis and had to move back in with her parents, two years had gone by since they'd last spoken. Kira hesitated to visit Miranda. At first it was because so much time had passed since they'd last spoken, she thought it would be awkward. After another three months went by without Kira making the trip to see her, Kira thought the gap between Miranda's initial diagnosis and any visit now would make things uncomfortable. After another two months, Kira learned

Miranda was confined to a wheelchair and unable to speak. Kira again hesitated because she was afraid to see Miranda in that condition. When Miranda died, Kira didn't go to the funeral because she was afraid of how people would react to her, since she'd never been out for a visit.

Although Kira was an expert at coming up with reasons not to visit her ailing friend, she's not alone in rationalizing hesitation. We all do it. Most often we rationalize our hesitancy by blaming timing. Maybe you say, "The time's not right." Your boss is just about to leave for lunch, so it's not a good time to bring up your new product idea. You'll wait to have children until you and your spouse have bought a home. It could be you think there's one perfect moment to take the action. Perhaps you resolve to sell your Microsoft shares when they peak in price. You'll take that trip to Tuscany when your business has turned the corner. A slight variation of this "time's not right" excuse is the "I'm not ready yet" justification. That's my favorite. I'm always preparing, and then preparing some more, and spending another weekend preparing, all to keep from facing a difficult task. Obsessive overpreparation is my form of procrastination.

Back when I was working out of my own small office (I'm currently a partner in a midsize firm), I faced a personnel crisis. I had an assistant who, it turned out, was less than candid. He would make mistakes, or forget matters, and then either hide them or cover them up with a web of superficially legitimate explanations. He was very outgoing and made sure to update me regularly about how his wife and newborn son were doing. He was solicitous and technically proficient. In hindsight, the signs of trouble were there early on—blaming others, disappearing documents—but I chose to ignore them, thinking he was just getting his bearings. Soon, however, clients began complaining about missed deadlines and definite mistakes. I knew I was facing a problem, but I hesitated to act. I knew the confrontation would be uncomfortable, so I decided first to gather information. My dossier started growing . . . but so did the problem. Then I began to rehearse my dialogue. It took a while to come up with the perfect language and commit it to memory. Next, I started putting a plan in place to deal with his departure, which hadn't yet happened, going so far as to line up a temporary replacement. Finally, I delayed so he could wrap up one particular matter and so I could prepare some clients for what was about to happen. I had spent more time preparing for this termination than I did studying for the bar exam decades earlier. When I could delay no longer, I finally "pulled the trigger." It wasn't an easy conversation, but it wasn't as difficult as I'd imagined. It turned out he had a history of this kind of behavior and knew it was only a matter of time before he'd be terminated again. I gained nothing by waiting for the perfect time to fire him. All I did by obsessively preparing and delaying was lose more sleep and money and clients than necessary.

Although I'm not ready to abandon all preparation, I do think there's something to be said for listening to your gut or heeding your inner voice. Philosophers such as Joseph Campbell have long argued for "following your bliss," citing spiritual notions. But in his recent book *Blink*, author Malcom Gladwell goes further, suggesting there may be a physical basis for accurate split-second decisions.° Gladwell believes there's a form of speed thinking called "thin-slicing," during which we draw conclusions based on slices of experience. Whatever its basis, I think it's better to seize a moment and act quickly than to procrastinate and lock fear in place.

°Little, Brown, 2005.

There's No Perfect Time

Besides, perfect timing is apparent only through hindsight. That's because time doesn't stand still and actions don't happen instantaneously. Let me explain.

Let's say you've decided to sell your shares of Acme Inc. at the moment they reach their top price. How will you know when that happens? When Acme Inc. is selling for $30 a share, you don't know whether it will soon jump to $35 or drop to $25. If you've resolved to wait for the perfect moment, you have to keep waiting. If it jumps to $35, you continue to wait since it could continue to climb. If it drops to $25, you continue to wait because it could soon jump back up to $30. People do the same thing with their real estate. Some folks who sold their homes in the summer of 2003 are now upset they didn't wait another six months since the market in their area kept rising. Others who haven't sold yet are now upset because the market in their area has slowed. The judgment of what is the perfect time for any action is knowable only after it has already passed.

That's not true just of economic decisions. Let's say you want to talk to your boss about an idea you have for a new service to offer customers. You want to discuss it with him at the perfect time. You're about to bring it up Wednesday afternoon but learn he's just gotten a call that one of your big customers canceled an order. You delay because you know he'll be upset. Your next window of opportunity is Friday afternoon, but you learn he wants to leave early to go away with his family for the weekend. You delay because you know he'll be impatient.

Or maybe you want to have a chat with your spouse about his temper with the kids. Once again, you want it to take place at the perfect time. You're ready to do it on Tuesday when he comes home from work. But he walks in the door and surprises you with a big bouquet of flowers. He wants to take you out to celebrate a big sale he closed that day. You don't want to spoil the evening, so you put it off. You're ready to have the conversation on Sunday afternoon, but he receives a call that a friend of his is very ill. You don't want to add to his burden.

Hesitancy is such a common problem that it's become a standard element in archetypal heroes. Uptight Clark Kent could never quite seem to find the right moment to tell Lois Lane that he's really Superman. Similarly, Peter Parker, the geeky teenager who's really Spider-Man, is always looking for the perfect time to tell the girl of his dreams, Mary Jane, the truth about his secret identity.° Something always comes along to keep the hero from telling the truth to his love. Actually, Clark and Peter always have some rationalization for putting off the conversations they're dreading. Nothing is getting in the way of their telling the truth other than their own fears. The lesson, I guess, is that even superheroes are afraid of failing.

If you're like me, the only superpower you possess is perfect hindsight. You will never know what was the perfect time to do something until after the time has passed. By continuing to believe there's a perfect time to do something, you ensure you'll delay taking the action. Not only that, but you guarantee you'll second-guess yourself afterward: "If only I had waited" or "If only I hadn't waited." And this type of self-criticism isn't the only pain you'll be experiencing.

> If you're like me, the only superpower you possess is perfect hindsight. You will never know what was the perfect time to do something until after the time has passed.

°Superman was created by Joe Shuster and Jerry Siegel. Spider-Man was created by Stan Lee.

Delayed Decisions Freeze Fear in Place

Fear is the reason we delay taking an action. We're afraid we're going to fail, or we're afraid of the unknown. The irony is that by delaying, we freeze the fear in place. And permanent fear leads to a kind of chronic emotional, psychological, and spiritual pain.

Let's say you're afraid of asking a man out to dinner because you're worried he'll turn you down. As a result, you delay asking him, rationalizing that the time isn't right. The longer you delay, the longer you will remain fearful of his rejection. As long as the outcome is in doubt, you are still frightened. That fear continues to lead you to delay. And since there's no perfect time, you can keep on rationalizing your inaction until he marries someone else. Then you can shrug it off, say it wasn't meant to be, and find someone else not to ask out to dinner. By delaying, you've locked your fear in place. It will be there to delay you the next time you meet someone and the time after that. By allowing this fear to take root, you are dooming yourself to the pain of loneliness. Only by taking the action and experiencing either success or failure can you get past this fear.

And it's not just the fear of failure that can be frozen in place; so can a fear of the unknown. Let's say you've delayed taking a foreign trip because you've never been overseas. You don't know what it will be like, and that's frightening. But as long as you keep from having the experience, keep from taking the action, it will remain unknown and, as a result, frightening. By allowing the fear to freeze in place, you don't take that semester in Stockholm during college, you don't take that vacation to Cologne, and you never go to visit your mother's family in Rome. If you don't face the fear and take the action, you are dooming yourself to a life filled with regrets and unfulfilled dreams. Only by making the unknown known can you get past this fear. The only way you can stop being afraid of traveling overseas is . . . traveling overseas.

The only way to stop feeling fearful is to take the action you're avoiding. Stop waiting for the perfect time; it will never come. Instead, realize that today is the best time to do anything. This is the moment. There's no time like now, so take the action. It may not always turn out positively, but at least you will put the fear behind you and be able to move on. There's a wonderful little story in the Talmud about a wise man walking in the countryside all by himself. He rounds a bend in the trail and comes upon a pack of wild dogs. Since he's afraid of dogs . . . he immediately sits down among them.

One of the hidden points in that parable is that the wise man "immediately" sits down among the dogs. He doesn't waste time worrying about what might happen or how things could turn out. He realizes every moment spent hesitating is another moment living in fear. He doesn't wait for the dogs to lie down to sleep, or to become distracted by a rabbit, or to start playing with one another. He realizes there's no perfect time to take the action. He knows the best time to take an action is now.

Getting Past Fears Means Getting Past Perfectionism

Sure, that's easier said than done. There's a big difference between some apocryphal wise man immediately sitting down among wild dogs and you actually having a frightening conversation with your boss.

The real-world secret to getting past your fears and taking action is to stop expecting perfection. John Henry Cardinal Newman warned that "a man would do nothing if he waited un-

til he could do it so well that no one could find fault." Many of
us hesitate and delay because we're afraid someone will find
fault with our actions, will judge us to be failures.

Why are we so afraid of failing? I think it's because we've
come to think that failing in an action makes us failures as human beings. We assume being a successful person means being
perfect. Success, even happiness, is equated with perfection.

If you want to see how obsessed we've become with perfection, just look at the offerings on television. There are shows
that tell us how to work out to perfect our physique. There are
shows that tell us what to wear and how to cut our hair. Other
shows offer up plastic surgery suggestions. Programs tell us how
to improve our sex lives, our parenting skills, and our pet's behavior. Experts remake our homes, our gardens, and our diets.
Nothing less than perfect is good enough in any aspect of our
lives.

Yet imperfection is what makes us human. The Hasidic rabbi
Elimelech Lizensker was once asked how he could be so sure
that he'd be welcomed in heaven. He said that when he stood
before the angels, they'd ask him, "Were you always a perfect
student?" He'd answer, "No." They'd then ask, "Were you entirely and completely scrupulous in your prayers and obser-
vance?" Again he'd answer, "No." Finally they'd ask: "Were you
always charitable and compassionate?" For a third time he'd
answer, "No." Then, he explained, the angels would welcome
him into heaven because he had spoken the truth. The angels
know that no one and nothing is perfect.

We all fail . . . often. I'm not a big baseball fan, but America's
pastime does offer us a wonderful example of how to view imperfection. An all-star hitter makes an out seven times out of
ten. If he succeeds more than 30 percent of the time over the
course of a long career, he could end up in the Hall of Fame.
Errors are an accepted part of the game, included up on the

scoreboard and in box scores. Pitchers are allowed to miss the strike zone three times without a batter being awarded a base. You can't follow a baseball game without accepting the imperfection of players. And you also can't lead a satisfied life without accepting your own imperfection and forgiving the imperfections of others. That includes spouses and parents and children and employees and employers and everyone else, not just baseball players.

There's a great episode of the television comedy *The Odd Couple**** in which Felix and Oscar, stressed out because of life in the city, decide to go on retreat to a monastery. There they are told to remain silent for twenty-four hours. Of course, they can't do it. When Felix asks the abbot what their punishment will be, he's told there is no punishment. The abbot tells Felix and Oscar that everyone fails and that in the future, when an employee or friend or family member fails one of the two men, perhaps they won't be as hard on that person.

When you're afraid of failing, you're actually afraid of living. The philosopher Epictetus believed that acknowledging imperfection is the first step to a full life: "To do anything well you must have the humility to bumble around a bit, to follow your nose, to get lost, to goof. Have the courage to try an undertaking and possibly do it poorly. Unremarkable lives are marked by the fear of not looking capable when trying something new." Frank Buchman, founder of the Oxford Group, which served as the basis for Alcoholics Anonymous and most of today's 12-step groups, preached a similar approach. His first step, and the first step in most of today's recovery programs, is the admission of personal defeat.

***Produced by Garry Marshall and starring Tony Randall as Felix and Jack Klugman as Oscar.

Unremarkable lives are marked by the fear of not looking
capable when trying something new.

—Epictetus

As long as you let the idea that you must be perfect keep you
from taking an action at which you could fail, or one that you've
never tried before, you won't be living up to your potential.
Give yourself permission to fail and you give yourself permission to succeed in life.

Learning to Fail

Football fans are so used to the ability of great offenses to exe-
cute on the field that they take it for granted. It's amazing that
eleven players can conduct intricate, almost balletic maneuvers
at lightning speed while eleven other equally skilled athletes
playing defense do all they can to disrupt the play. How do they
accomplish this amazing feat? Practice. Players spend much of
their off-season working together and running through scenar-
ios. The practice continues throughout the season and even
into pregame warm-ups. To learn how to fail, you need to take
a lesson from football players. You should practice.

I doubt William James would have been much of an offensive
coordinator, but he'd agree with football players' dedication to
practice. James suggested a great way to learn how to overcome
fear of failure and its resulting hesitation:"Keep the faculty of
effort alive in you by a little gratuitous exercise every day. That
is, be systematically ascetic or heroic in little unnecessary points,
do every day or two something for no other reason than that
you would rather not do it, so that when the hour of dire need
draws nigh, it may find you not unnerved and untrained to

stand the test." Ralph Waldo Emerson had a similar idea: "He has not learned the lesson of life who does not every day surmount a fear."

He has not learned the lesson of life who does not every day surmount a fear.

—Ralph Waldo Emerson

If you're a very systematic, determined individual, you can sit down and come up with a list of actions, large and small, that you've hesitated to undertake. Perhaps you've been putting off calling your aunt whose birthday you missed. Maybe you've hesitated to talk to your assistant about her repeated lateness. Or it could be you've delayed making an appointment for a complete physical until you've lost weight. Having drawn up your list, make a concerted and proactive effort to tackle one action each day for the next week. Prioritize the items by difficulty . . . and then do the most difficult one first. By overcoming the biggest of the obstacles right away, you turn this "heroic" exercise into a downhill glide rather than an uphill slog.

Although this kind of shock therapy can be very effective, it can also be hard to adopt. That's one reason you might prefer what I call the reflexive approach. All this requires is an awareness of the fact that you're putting something off or hesitating. The moment you realize you don't want to do something, do it. It doesn't matter if it's something large, like asking your boss for time off, or something minor, like emptying the dishwasher. Rather than put something off, do it immediately. Find out you need to make a condolence visit? Do it that night. Discover you've got to call a client and tell him about a mistake? Pick up the telephone right then. Need to talk to your son about his failing grade in chemistry? Do it as soon as you get home from work. When you make a to-do list for household chores, do the most onerous task first. At work, when you prepare your call list for the next day, put the one you're most dreading at the top and make that your first call of the next day. The idea is to turn instant undaunted action into a habit.

Don't focus on the end result of the action. Instead, concentrate on the action itself. That's what you have control over. Success comes from taking an action, not from a positive outcome. Failure comes through hesitation, not a negative outcome. Of course you want positive outcomes. But life isn't always positive. Teach yourself to take actions and not spend so much time worrying about results.

There's a great scene in Larry McMurtry's book *Lonesome Dove** in which the cowboy Augustus offers advice like this to his friend Call. Augustus criticizes Call for never wanting to admit he's wrong and says that, personally, he's glad he's wrong so often. Call can't understand why. Augustus explains that since no one is perfect, you may as well get used to it. If you're wrong only a couple of times in life, those incidents will be very upsetting. But if you're wrong once or twice every day, you get so used to it that being right or wrong won't matter so much.

When during the course of your day-to-day life you find yourself hesitating or rationalizing inaction, ask yourself what you're afraid of. Then get past your fear of failure by taking the action.

"I'm Afraid It Will Cause a Rift in the Family"

Sarah Harford, fifty-four, knew she needed to speak with her younger sister, Cheryl, about their mother Rachel's finances and health care. Rachel, seventy-six, wasn't doing well physi-

*Simon & Schuster, 1985.

cally or financially. Still living in the same apartment in which she'd raised her family, Rachel was having a hard time caring for herself. She rarely went out—"I get tired just going downstairs, and there's nothing out there for me anyway"—and didn't seem to be eating well or taking her medications regularly. When Sarah broached the issue of moving to an assisted living facility, her mother shot it down immediately. Cheryl supported their mother's objections—because of her own denial, in Sarah's opinion. Then Sarah suggested hiring an aide to come in for a few hours every day to help out. Her mother said she couldn't afford it, and Cheryl had no comment.

Sarah knew Cheryl and her husband, Tom, weren't doing well financially. Tom had lost his job and was having a hard time finding another. Sarah was afraid Cheryl would get defensive about her finances. The disparity between the two sisters' financial situations was a touchy issue. The sisters had been estranged for a number of years after a fight over money, and Sarah didn't want that to happen again. Part of Sarah wanted to wait to bring it up until Tom got another job. Maybe, she thought, she should wait until after Easter, so there wasn't a family rift around the holiday.

Sarah knew delay would only lock her own fear in place and potentially harm her mother. She picked up the telephone and called Cheryl. It didn't go well. As Sarah expected, Cheryl got defensive and struck out at Sarah. The two sisters snapped at each other as if they were teenagers again, and Cheryl hung up the phone. Sarah's fears had been realized. But, ironically, that night she slept well for the first time in months. There was no longer an ax hanging above her head. Sarah had lived with the fear of a rift with her sister. Now that it had happened, she was no longer afraid of it. She knew where they stood. Sarah was now facing an actual obstacle—arranging for her mother's care—rather than just a fear.

The next day, Cheryl phoned back and was calmer. She admitted that she and her husband couldn't afford to help Rachel financially. Sarah suggested that rather than contributing money, Cheryl could contribute time, making sure to go over to Rachel's apartment three days a week, while Sarah would pay for an aide to come in the other four days. Cheryl agreed. Things aren't perfect between the sisters and their mother. There are still snags and disagreements. But that's family life.

"I'll Start Looking Again When the Industry Picks Up"

That was Liam Martin's reflexive first reaction to his inability to find a job after two months. An experienced copy editor, Liam, thirty-four, had been terminated from his job at a company that published trade magazines in the computer and office technology industries. He started looking for another copy-editing job in the magazine industry less than a week after being fired. But he soon found not only that other magazines weren't hiring, but that the rest of the magazine industry was trimming staff as well. Liam had gotten married two years earlier. His wife, Deb, thirty-two, was working as a part-time fact checker for an entertainment magazine and was also taking courses for her master's degree. They didn't make much money, but they'd managed to save enough for a couple of months' rent or a much needed vacation.

Liam knew he was good at what he did and had never before had a problem finding work. But he could see that Deb, while outwardly sounding confident, was worried about their situation. Liam tried to reassure her by saying he was sure the magazine industry would pick up again soon. Meanwhile, they could draw on their savings if need be to get through the summer. Instead of providing comfort for Deb, that just made her more nervous. Liam was about to say that even if the industry didn't pick up soon, there were bound to be openings in the fall, but something in Deb's eyes made him keep quiet. In a shaking voice, she asked, "Don't you think maybe you should look for something outside the magazine business?"

Liam was going to argue with her, but something clicked. He realized the reason he was thinking of taking time off from his job search was that he was afraid of looking for work in another industry. He had worked in publishing since graduating college and didn't know if or how his skills would fit in a different industry. Liam realized that hesitating to broaden his job search would only freeze his fear in place. And besides keeping his fears alive, it would also threaten their financial life.

After a few moments, he told Deb she was right. While he'd like to get back into the magazine industry, he'd stop counting on it. He told her he'd scour the entire classified section of the next day's paper, activate his whole network, and make appointments with some temp agencies as well.

Even doing all that, it took Liam another six weeks to find a job. It was a position in a public relations agency, creating media kits and writing press releases. It wasn't his dream job, but it paid just about the same as his job at the magazine. After eighteen months he's still at the agency, but he continues to look out for any magazine jobs that open up.

"I Don't Want to Make Him Angry"

Andrea Duffy, forty-four, was growing increasingly worried about her husband, Sean, forty-five. A high school administrator at a midsize suburban school, Sean had been drinking more than usual. It wasn't that he was getting drunk all the time. It was just that, after having maybe one or two drinks a week for decades, he was now having a couple of Scotch and sodas every day as soon as he came home from work. At first, Andrea chalked it up to Sean's having a particularly troublesome class that year at the school. But then Sean started sleeping in for a long time on the weekends and becoming irritable every Sunday night. The past couple of weeks he'd been very short-tempered with the kids, Bobby, twelve, and Liz, eight.

Andrea had tried talking to Sean about it a couple of times, but he'd either cut her short or joked that it was just a midlife crisis. When, at a family barbecue, Andrea mentioned Sean's behavior to his older sister, Wendy, she saw Wendy's eyes start to well up. "That sounds just like our father," Wendy said. "We spent years ignoring our father's depression, and it made a mess of all of us. You really should get Sean to talk to someone."

On the drive home from the barbecue, Andrea started playing out the conversation with Sean in her mind. She initially thought of having it that night, after the kids had gone to bed. But then she thought it might be better to wait until after the school board meeting on Wednesday. Actually, maybe they should talk next Friday; that way they could hammer it out over the weekend. As Andrea kept thinking of the perfect time to have the conversation with Sean, she realized she was rationalizing her delay. She asked herself what she was afraid of. Andrea realized she was afraid of Sean's anger being turned on her.

Sean was quick-witted and sharp-tongued. Usually this came out in a winning sense of humor, but when he was angry it came out in very cutting, hurtful comments. She'd seen him react that way with his sisters and mother in the past. Andrea knew if she kept putting off the conversation, she'd lock this fear of Sean's anger in place and it would end up being a cancer, eating away their relationship. She resolved to talk to him that evening when the kids were in bed.

Andrea did just that. Sean did get angry and started lashing out verbally, but when Andrea told him he was treating her the same way he treated his mother and sisters, he backed off and started to listen. It wasn't an easy or pleasant conversation, and it went on well past midnight. But by the end of the evening, Sean agreed to set up an appointment with a psychotherapist.

Choose Hope over Fear

Once you take an action, whatever the result, you'll be free of that fear. You won't lead a fearless life; that's not the goal. Fear is part of life for most of us. It's the rare person who's a hero, who has the courage to not feel fear. Most of us need to, in the words of the author Susan Jeffers, feel the fear and do it anyway. Stop striving to be fearless. Instead, strive to be dauntless. To be happy, you need to accept your fears and the limitations of being human and get on with it. Sometimes you'll win, sometimes you'll lose, but at least you'll be in the game of life rather than hesitating on the sidelines like a spectator. You'll be happy today. Confront your fear. Realize there's no time like now. And take the action.

> To be happy, you need to accept your fears and the limitations of being human and get on with it. Sometimes you'll win, sometimes you'll lose, but at least you'll be in the game of life rather than hesitating on the sidelines like a spectator.

Sarah, Liam, and Andrea are no more courageous than any of the rest of us. Faced with having to take an action, they were all tempted to hesitate, to delay, to procrastinate, in order to avoid failure or the unknown. But they knew that if they gave in to their fear, it would lodge in their souls and bring pain and un-happiness. Instead, they chose to be dauntless. When you live undaunted, you'll be better able to reach your goals and achieve your dreams. You'll lead a life guided by hopes rather than fears. I think the novelist Joseph Conrad put it best: "Facing it—always facing it—that's the way to get through. Face it!"

There's No Time Like Now, So Take the Action

- We all hesitate to take actions or make decisions, in matters large and small, occasionally or regularly, and as a result delay potential success and freeze our fears in place.
- Sometimes we hesitate because we believe there's a perfect time to take an action. But we'll never know the perfect time until it has passed.
- Other times we hesitate because we're afraid of failure or the unknown. But hesitancy only locks fear in place, leading to chronic emotional, psychological, and spiritual pain.
- We need to stop expecting perfection in timing or results; it's imperfection that makes us human. Fear of failure is fear of living. When we give ourselves permission to fail, we give ourselves permission to succeed.
- The moment we realize we're hesitating to take an action, we need to take that action. We need to make action habitual.
- We needn't try to be fearless—fear is part of life. Instead, we need to be dauntless.

(7)

YOUR BEST IS ENOUGH

You can't have everything. Where would you
put it?

—*Steven Wright*

t's okay if you leave the office at 5:00 p.m. Don't sweat it if
your abs resemble a keg rather than a six-pack. And it's all
right if your retirement fund isn't worth more than your
home. What matters is that you do your best, not that you have
the perfect career, the perfect body, or the perfect portfolio.

Being happy, having a good life that provides emotional, psychological, and spiritual fulfillment and satisfaction, means realizing it's impossible to have everything. Sure, you can try, but
you'll not only be unhappy, you'll probably end up with a migraine from repeatedly banging your head against a wall. Contentment comes when you set priorities and play the hand
you've been dealt the best you can. Happiness comes from a
well-rounded life.

Being happy, having a good life that provides emotional, psychological, and spiritual fulfillment and satisfaction, means realizing it's impossible to have everything.

Aspiring to Be the Best

Unfortunately, most people don't seem to know that today. We're living at a time when your best isn't enough; you need to aspire to be *the* best.

It's not enough to have a job, you need to have a career: a planned long-term work path providing satisfaction, a top income, and status and enabling you to "make a difference."

It's not enough to be healthy and fit, you need to have your optimal body mass index, the physique of a body builder, and the aerobic capacity of a marathoner.

It's not enough to have a happy marriage, you need to be as "connected" as conjoined twins and have mind-blowing sex three times a week.

It's not enough to be a good parent who raises good kids in a nice home, you need to be a combination Mr. Rogers and Martha Stewart raising a child who's equal parts Mozart, Einstein, and Tiger Woods in a home that rivals Versailles.

It's not enough to save as much as you can, you need to invest half your income so brilliantly that you can send your kid to Yale, hire a live-in caregiver for your mother, and retire to a luxury condo in the Sunbelt . . . early.

It's not enough to be able to make dinner for your family, you need to be a gourmet chef. It's not enough to have clean, appropriate clothing, you need to be a fashionista. It's not enough to have a vehicle that's safe and reliable, you need to drive a Navigator with a Mini towed behind as a lifeboat.

And most insane of all, you need to do and have all of the above. Anything less and you're not living up to your potential; you're not having the best life.

Okay, I'm exaggerating some, but not a lot. I'm constantly amazed at how pressured people are to have and do it all. Granted, as a resident of New York City I'm exposed to an unusually driven and trendy population. But from what I can see, the difference between such people and the average American is only one of degree. New Yorkers aren't any more obsessed with having everything; what they want is just a bit more expensive.

While the need to have everything is epidemic today, this self-defeating urge has been around for centuries. There's a wonderful Sufi story about two friends who are catching up after not seeing each other for some time. One is married, the other single. The married man asks his single buddy about his love life. The single friend explains that a few months ago he thought he had found the perfect woman. "She had a gorgeous face," he says. "Her body was incredible."

"So why didn't you marry her?" his friend asks.

"Well," explains the single friend, "she wasn't very intelligent." He goes on to explain that a few weeks later he found another woman he thought was perfect. "She was as beautiful as the first woman, and brilliant as well."

"So why didn't you marry this woman?" his friend asks.

"Well, she had a voice that sounded like nails on a blackboard."

The married friend nods, but before he can say anything the single friend continues: "Then, just last week I finally met the perfect woman. She's beautiful, she's intelligent, and her voice is soothing and relaxing."

"So when's the wedding?" the married friend asks.

"There won't be one," the single friend explains. "It turns out she's looking for the perfect man."

"I Need to Become the Top Salesperson"

Barbara Reagan, a tiny forty-six-year-old woman who still looks like the gymnast she once was, is driven to succeed. When she graduated college and became an elementary school teacher, she strove to be the best and succeeded. Named "Teacher of the Year" three times at her own school, she went on to win the award from her home state and was named a finalist for the national award. It was only after feeling she had nothing else to prove as a classroom teacher that Barbara decided to take a job with a company that sells computerized reading systems to school districts. With firsthand experience of a classroom teacher's needs and wants, she was quickly able to establish good relations with most of the districts in her region. After three years on the job, her sales figures were fine—just where they were projected by the company. But she lagged behind two other staffers in the company, both of whom were longtime salespeople rather than former teachers.

Unhappy about her progress, Barbara had a heart-to-heart chat with the company's national sales manager, who suggested she attend some training courses as well as alter her approach to sales. Barbara wasn't used to socializing after hours. She worked hard as a teacher, but that meant staying after school a few afternoons a week. She was always home in time for dinner with her husband, Brian, and their two girls and was almost never away overnight or on weekends. In addition, since she taught in the same district in which her daughters—Carrie, sixteen, and Jeannie, thirteen—went to school, she was always there for their afterschool events. Brian's accounting office was near home, so any events Barbara couldn't attend, he was able to cover. A day after Barbara's conversation with her sales manager, she sat down with Brian and the girls and explained that she'd be spending more time on the road. No one was happy about it, but they were outwardly supportive.

Barbara's new approach began to generate results within a couple of months. Unfortunately, they weren't all positive. While her sales increased a bit, things at home were difficult. Brian did his best to pick up the slack for her increased absences, but he couldn't be in two places at once. Occasionally, he was forced to choose between conflicting events in the two girls' lives, which meant one of them would be unhappy. Things came to a head when Barbara was out of town overnight on a sales meeting with a prospective customer. Brian went to a play-off game of Carrie's volleyball team, leaving no one to attend Jeannie's dance recital. She was inconsolable and remained so even after Barbara came home the next day. "Honey," Barbara tried to explain, "I need to become the top salesperson."

"I Need to Break 3:15"

Chris Graves, forty-one, is obsessed with the New York City Marathon. For most of her life, Chris had been overweight. Unpopular in high school and college, she dedicated herself to academics. Despite outstanding grades, she didn't have the confidence to apply to law schools, as her professors suggested, and instead trained as a paralegal. After working for almost eight years at a large firm, Chris was pushed by the partners there to go to law school. She was so highly thought of by the firm that it not only pushed for her acceptance at a prestigious local college, but helped with the tuition. While at school, a female professor took Chris under her wing and prodded her not just to study, but to lose weight and dress more fashionably. Chris began exercising and dieting religiously. By the time she graduated law school, she was sixty pounds lighter. When she returned to the law firm, now as an associate, she was barely recognized by the partners and staff.

What didn't change, however, was Chris's dedication. Now it encompassed not just her work, but her fitness program. Chris had seen her life and self-image turn around, and she swore she'd never go back. Inspired by another runner at the firm, Chris decided to enter an upcoming marathon. But finishing wasn't enough of a goal, she wanted to finish under 3:15. Told that would be extraordinary for a first-time marathoner, she wasn't dissuaded. In fact, it motivated her more. Chris ran each morning before work and then trained at a gym after work. In the evening, she had just enough time to shower and have dinner before going to bed so she could get up in time for her morning run. Every weekend she went for a long run as well.

Work and fitness left Chris with little time for socializing. Most of her personal life revolved around her large extended family. Early in November, Chris's mother told her the family has decided to hold a Thanksgiving reunion at the upstate farm that has been in the family for generations. Chris explained she couldn't take that much time off work, and besides, she didn't want to cut short her training program. Her mother couldn't believe Chris would pass on the family reunion. "Mom," Chris tried to explain, "I need to break 3:15."

"We Need to Have More Set Aside"

Mike Everett, fifty-one, has always been a planner. His casual exterior—a salt-and-pepper beard and long gray hair pulled back into a ponytail—belies his disciplined nature. Years ago, when he and his wife, Violet, now fifty, were planning to move from their first apartment to a new home, he started packing before they'd even found a house. Mike has created a shopping list template for trips to the supermarket that matches the layout of the store. A scratch golfer, Mike has kept exhaustive volumes of notes on local courses. Their CD collection is alphabetized, and the storage boxes in the garage are all labeled. Violet jokes that if she and the dogs sit still for too long, Mike will label them as well. While he joins in the jokes about his planning, Mike takes pride in having been organized enough to have built up two businesses and a nice financial nest egg.

Both he and Violet are self-employed; he's an acupuncturist, and she's a massage therapist. To launch their own businesses, they needed to be prudent with their money. Mike, who always enjoyed money matters, took charge of their joint finances. They've done well enough that they can take biannual foreign vacations, which they love. Now, with both of their businesses pretty well established and with no children to worry about, Mike has begun to plan for retirement. Once their business debts were paid off, Mike sat with a financial planner to set up retirement plans for both him and Violet. Over the years, despite fluctuations in their incomes, they've put away as much money in tax-deferred plans as the law allowed. But this year, money is tighter than before.

The largest employer in their community, a technology company involved in telecommunications, recently laid off quite a few people. The ripple effect has been felt by most businesses in the small city, including Mike's and Violet's. Although they've been able to meet all their personal and business bills, afterward, they've very little disposable money left. It has been two years since their last vacation, and Violet has been looking into a hiking trip in the Scottish Highlands. Mike is less than enthusiastic, and when Violet called him on it, he admitted his hesitation: "We need to put more money aside."

The Numbers Giveth . . .

Barbara, Chris, Mike, and the rest of us haven't always been this way. This drive to have everything actually began with the baby boom generation. Boomers have had, and continue to have, an unprecedented impact on our society and culture, and this has had an effect on other generations as well. All of us—seniors, boomers, Gen X'ers, and Gen Y'ers—have now bought into it.

As I noted in an earlier chapter, the baby boom is the largest generation in history: about seventy-six million, according to most estimates. Owing to its size, the baby boom generation has had an extraordinary impact. For example, suburbs were developed to give boomers homes, safe communities in which to grow up, and lots of schools. Boomer tastes and fashions and trends have become, by default, the national tastes, fashions, and trends. When the single largest demographic bloc decides blue jeans and T-shirts are the fundamentals in a wardrobe, they fill the national closet. What boomers listen to, read, eat, and think forms the foundation of popular culture. Other generations, before and since, have had to carve out places for themselves in society. On the other hand, society changes to fit boomers.

This hasn't been an entirely negative process. Most of the indisputably positive social trends of the past three to four decades come straight out of the baby boom: racial and gender equality, environmentalism, health awareness, and the search for spirituality, to name just four. And thanks to the influence of boomers, those trends have also seen widespread adoption by other generational groups. But baby boomers have also been responsible for spawning and spreading the national obsession with wanting everything. Once again, it has to do with numbers.

Because the baby boom generation is so large, and because a society with unprecedented wealth and power—post–World War II America—was catering to its needs when they were growing up, they were viewed as the generation that would "fix" the world. Parents who weathered the Depression and war and who, as a result, felt they may not have been able to live up to their potential, were going to ensure that their kids had every opportunity. Boomers grew up being told they could do anything and be anything; that the only limit on their future was their own imagination. Instinctively, it seemed to be true. After all, communities, industries, and society as a whole were changing in response to the needs and wants of baby boomers. Boomers believed they won the vote, liberated women, and ended an unpopular war. But just as the baby boom generation's potential for having everything came from its numbers, so does its inability to reach that potential.

. . . And the Numbers Taketh Away

The more slices you cut out of a pie, the smaller is each portion. Sure, you could bake a bigger pie to compensate, but when so many unexpected guests arrive so quickly, you don't have time for that. That's what happened with baby boomers: seventy-six million unexpected guests arrived at once, and the American economy and society simply couldn't expand fast enough to provide them all with the opportunities to which they were told they were entitled.

More baby boomers went to college than any other generation. It wasn't just their overall size; more women went to college than ever before. And while the higher education industry expanded to make room for all these new students, the sheer numbers of college diplomas being issued led to a devaluation of bachelor's degrees. College graduates no longer automatically got top jobs, since they weren't a rare elite. The elite were those with postgraduate or professional degrees. Getting those master's degrees, or going to law school, for example, usually required going into debt.

More baby boomers went into the job market than any other generation. Once again, it wasn't just overall numbers; more women were going into the workplace than ever before. American business responded in the same manner as American higher education, creating all sorts of lower- and middle-level management positions. But with so many people in the bureaucracy, there weren't as many opportunities to move up the ladder. And with payrolls now so large, companies could no longer afford to keep salaries and benefits at the same level. Real income stagnated, and perquisites like defined benefit pensions became extinct.

More baby boomers entered the real estate market than any other generation. Yet again, it wasn't just the overall numbers, but the readiness of single male and female baby boomers and couples without children to purchase co-ops and condominiums as well as detached single-family homes. While home building and development soared to try to keep pace, it wasn't enough. The incredible demand for the limited supply of housing drove prices up to record levels in the 1980s—they've never really fallen since. Although that was wonderful news for my generation, the parents of boomers—who used the profits made by selling our homes to your generation to finance our retirements—it made purchasing a home more of a financial burden for boomers and subsequent generations than it was for me and my peers.

Now, as baby boomers grow older, more people will be retiring than ever before. While that will without doubt change the way we view retirement and senior citizens—the changes are already starting—it will also necessarily stretch Social Security and Medicare into different shapes.

What's clear is that the economic reality that comes with being such a large generation makes it incredibly difficult for boomers and younger generations to replicate the lifestyle of the fifties, sixties, and seventies, even with both spouses working. You can indeed have anything—there are fewer barriers to individual advancement and opportunity than ever before—but you can't have everything. You simply don't have the money.

It's not just the money; you don't have the time, either. Life may be getting increasingly complex, but there are still only twenty-four hours in a day and seven days in a week. There aren't enough hours in the day to devote yourself to your career, family, and fitness. There aren't enough days in the week for you to devote yourself to managing the growth of your portfolio, soul, and garden. To become the best in any one area will require you to give short shrift to other areas. If you want to be a world-famous violinist, you're not going to have the time to micromanage your investments and pick up your son at school every day.

You Can't Get Orange Juice from a Coconut

There are a handful of people for whom single-minded devotion to one aspect of their lives at the expense of everything else will lead to happiness and fulfillment. I think of them as savants; they're people whose brains are wired so specifically for one aspect of life, they can get all they need from pursuing it. But I think most of us achieve contentment from having a more multifaceted life, one in which we do the best we can in a number of different areas by making compromises and choices. Saint Augustine once famously asked, "What am I then, my

God? What is my nature?" The answer he received was, "A life varied, multifaceted, and truly immense."

The quest for personal fulfillment doesn't have a simple solution. Not only isn't there a magic bullet that works for everyone, but it takes more than one bullet for almost everyone to be happy. "The heart, like the stomach, wants a varied diet," wrote Gustave Flaubert. I think the psychologist Abraham Maslow probably did the best job of outlining just how varied a diet.

> The heart, like the stomach, wants a varied diet.
> —Gustave Flaubert

Maslow theorized we all have five types of needs. Our most basic needs are physiological, like oxygen, water, food, sleep, and sex. Then we have safety and security needs, such as having a safe home, job security, and savings. Next are love and belonging needs. That's where marriage, family, friends, and community come in. Then there are esteem needs. These are things like status, respect, recognition, confidence, and mastery over what we do. Finally, there are self-actualization needs like creativity, beauty, uniqueness, order, self-sufficiency, and meaningfulness. Maslow believed people addressed their needs in this order. In other words, you wouldn't seek to meet your esteem needs until you'd addressed your love and belonging needs. Setting aside the validity of his other ideas, what's important for us is that Maslow divided human needs into distinct categories. I don't think you can expect any one aspect of your life—be it career, family, finance, fitness, or hobby—to address all those needs.

In a capitalist society, work is primarily an income-generating process. Its purpose is to make you money, not provide you with purpose. "The blessing of life as a whole," noted the philosopher Hannah Arendt, "can never be found in work." You need the money work provides to help you meet your basic physiological and safety needs. Your workplace may or may not also help meet some of your needs for esteem and belonging. But it's not in its nature to meet your needs for beauty and meaningfulness. "Work though we must," noted author Melinda Marshall, "our jobs do not automatically determine our priorities concerning our marriages, our children, our social life, or even our health. It's still life, constrained as it may be by limited disposable income or leisure time, and we're still responsible for making it something we enjoy or endure." Yet many of us devote most of our waking hours to work in the hope that it will somehow provide most of our nonmonetary needs.

The film *Lost in Translation*° offers a fascinating look at what happens when personal needs are sacrificed for career advancement. Bob Harris, played by Bill Murray, is an aging American action film star who's visiting Tokyo to appear in a whiskey commercial. Charlotte, played by Scarlett Johansson, is a recent college graduate who's in Tokyo with her professional photographer husband, John, played by Giovanni Ribisi. John's drive to advance his career leads him to ignore Charlotte. As a result, she spends most of her time with Bob. In the past, Bob had made a choice similar to John's, leading to his now unhappy marriage. Aging baby boomer Bob now realizes the mistake of having chosen work over personal life and sees the younger John and Charlotte repeating the same pattern.

While expecting work to fill all your needs is a mistake, it's also self-defeating to expect that your needs for esteem and creativity will be filled through family and friends. We all know parents whose own self-esteem is derived from the achieve-

°Written and directed by Sofia Coppola.

ments of their children. That's not a baby boomer–created phenomenon. More than a century ago, Ralph Waldo Emerson wrote: "I suffer whenever I see that common sight of a parent or senior imposing his opinion and way of thinking and being on a young soul to which they are totally unfit. Cannot we let people be themselves, and enjoy life in their own way? You are trying to make another man you. One's enough."

Less obvious than pushy parents are those whose needs for creativity and freedom are stifled by their family obligations. In the incredibly powerful book *The Hours*,* by Michael Cunningham, the character Laura Brown is a pregnant housewife in the 1950s who feels spiritual and emotional despair at being a stay-at-home wife and mother. Her husband is loving and happy. Her son is intelligent and artistic. Her home is lovely. Yet she's in psychic torment. She comes close to suicide before deciding to abandon her family. As she explains at the end of the book, "I chose to live." Suicide and abandonment are extreme reactions, but the problem is real. "To get time for civic work, for exercise, for neighborhood projects, reading or meditation, or just plain time to themselves, mothers need to hold out against the fairly recent but surprisingly entrenched myth that 'good mothers' are constantly with their children," urged author Wendy Coppedge Sanford. "They will have to speak out at last about the demoralizing effect of spending day after day with small children, no matter how much they love them."

I always tell people you can't get orange juice from a coconut. Trying will only drive you crazy. That's what I think you're doing when, for instance, you try to meet spiritual needs through work. Look to work for safety and security and esteem. Look to family and community for love and belonging and meaning-

---

*Farrar, Straus & Giroux, 1998.

fulness. Look to your hobbies and pastimes for creativity and beauty.

Look to work for safety and security and esteem. Look to family and community for love and belonging and meaningfulness. Look to your hobbies and pastimes for creativity and beauty.

Expanding Your Reach by Reining in Your Dreams

Rather than look to one aspect of your life to meet all or even most of your needs, expand your reach. Give time and energy to the varied aspects of your life that you know will give you the best opportunity to meet your different needs. To achieve contentment, we need to make compromises and choices. "Nothing is certain in life," wrote social psychologist Faye J. Crosby, "but generally the chances of happiness are greater if one has multiple areas of interest and involvement. To juggle is to diminish the risk of depression, anxiety, and unhappiness." David Allen, one of today's foremost thinkers on personal productivity, believes, "We suffer the stress of infinite opportunity: There are so many things we could do, and all we see are people who seem to be performing at star quality. It's very hard not to try to be like them. The problem is, if you get wrapped up in that game, you'll get eaten alive. You can do anything—but not everything. The universe is full of creative projects that are waiting to be done. So, if you really care about quality of life, if you want to relax, then don't focus on values. Just control your aspirations. That will simplify things." That will also lead to happiness.

The chances of happiness are greater if one has multiple areas of interest and involvement. To juggle is to diminish the risk of depression, anxiety, and unhappiness.

—Faye J. Crosby

In order to control your aspirations, you'll need to do some thinking and soul-searching. You'll need to decide which of your aspirations in life are taking up too much of your time and energy and leading you to shortchange other aspirations in your life. That's certainly not a simple task. Nor is it one I think you can accomplish in an hour. That being said, I think it's important for me to give you some kind of formal and finite process to at least get you started.

Make yourself a pot of tea or coffee, or if you prefer, pour a glass of wine. Find a comfortable, quiet place where you'll be able to sit and think for at least an hour. Take out your journal and turn to a blank left-hand page so you have two blank pages face-to-face. On top of the left-hand page write the words "The Best." On top of the right-hand page write the words "My Best."

On the left-hand side of the left-hand page, list the important areas of your life. Skip two or three lines between each item. For instance, you might write "career" on the first line, "relationship" on the fourth, "children" on the seventh, "retirement" on the tenth, "house" on the thirteenth, "cooking" on the sixteenth, and "travel" on the nineteenth. Don't worry about putting the items in any particular order. Just write them down as they come to mind. In addition, don't feel that any are too insignificant to mention. If you play "golf," put that down. If you want to lose weight, write "diet." It's better to have too many than to leave anything out.

Obviously, if you realize later on that you've forgotten something, you can add it. If you have to start another page, go ahead. Also, remember you're writing this list for your own benefit. No one, not even me, is going to see this list, so don't fall into the trap of writing what you think should be important to you or not including something you're afraid others wouldn't consider important. If collecting toy soldiers is an important part of your life, write it down. And if you're a loner and really don't care about your social life, don't feel pressure to include it on your list. Once you have a list you feel confident represents most, if not all, of the important areas in your life, you can move on to the next step.

Consider the first item on your list. What would it mean for you to be the best in that area of your life? What would it take? For instance, if you wrote down "career," what would being the best mean: a salary of $150,000? What would it take for you to achieve that: working twelve-hour days? Work your way down your list, noting your ultimate goal for each area in your life and what you think it would take to get there. Perhaps you want to lose fifty pounds to get back to the weight you were before your marriage, and that would mean a restricted diet and ninety minutes at the gym six days a week. Once you've sketched all this out, go over your notes. Based on what you've written, would it be possible to achieve more than one of these goals? Or would you need to focus on just one area of your life to achieve your ultimate goal?

Now turn to the right-hand page you headed "My Best." Assume you need to incorporate all these areas into your life. With your time and energy therefore at a premium, what would be the minimum achievement you'd look for in each area? What would it take to achieve that minimum satisfactory goal? Let's say you lower your salary demand to $75,000. Could you earn that by working nine to five? It could be that rather than losing fifty pounds, you'd accept losing ten. Could you achieve that by cutting back on your desserts and snacks and exercising for sixty minutes three times a week?

Once you've actually analyzed the difference between being the best and doing your best, look to incorporate the lessons into your life. Resolve to set aside some time each day, or each week, to each of the areas of your life you've listed as important. Make obvious allowances for the time of year—you don't need to tend your garden in November or go skiing in April— but try to spend at least some time every day or week on each area of importance. This will force you to choose between, let's say, staying late at the office on a Friday or going to the theater with your spouse. You'll need to decide whether you'd rather spend an hour more at the health club each day or be home in time to cook dinner for the family.

Think of these choices as addition by subtraction. You're adding to your happiness by giving up the drive to be the best at everything. Figure out all the things that are important to you, and do the best you can in each. You can't give 100 percent effort to anything, unless there's nothing else in your life. It's fine to give 40 percent effort to your teaching career, and 50 percent effort to your wife and daughter, and 10 percent effort to playing the guitar . . . or any other division of effort into any number of areas in your life. These aren't sacrifices. The only thing you'll be losing is your frustration.

You can't give 100 percent effort to anything, unless there's nothing else in your life.

Incidentally, people often find that by reining in their dreams, they not only become happier, but actually achieve more in the individual areas of their lives. Sometimes less really is more. Your best performance may come after you've decided you don't need to give 110 percent and you remove the pressure for perfection.

"Making My Quota Is Fine"

Barbara Reagan feels terrible about missing her daughter's dance recital. But she also thinks her daughter is overreacting. It isn't as if Barbara has made a practice of missing her girls' events. For most of their lives, she's been far more a part of their extracurricular activities than other parents. Barbara knows this was just her youngest daughter's way of expressing her anger over the changes in their lifestyle, but she thinks it raises an important issue.

While she was a teacher, it was easy for Barbara to devote lots of energy to her career. The hours fit very well into her daughters' lives. Barbara was able to be there for her girls and do what she thought necessary to be the best teacher. Her new job doesn't give her the chance to do both. She is going to have to make some choices.

Later that week, she had a rare chance to be alone. The girls were at friends' houses and Brian was out playing racquetball. Barbara asked herself why she needed to be the top salesperson at the company. Was it for the extra money? Not really. With two girls going to college, every penny certainly helped, but they were doing just fine already. Was it for the recognition? No. That would be nice, but it wasn't very important to her. It really was for her own ego. She wanted to prove to herself that she could be the best at this, just as she was the best at teaching. In that case, was it worth what she'd have to give up?

Barbara didn't decide to give up her job and become a stay-at-home mom. But she did choose to rein in her goals. She is going to take the sales seminars her manager suggested, but she isn't going to go out of her way to take extensive overnight business trips. She'll do all she can to be home as much as she can. She may not be able to be home for every event, and she may not be able to schedule all her sales meetings at her clients' convenience. She'll do the best she can: "Making my quota is fine."

"Just Finishing Is Okay"

Chris Graves never did make it to her family's Thanksgiving reunion. She worked late in the office Wednesday and then decided to go for a long run on Thanksgiving Day. Taking her usual route through the park, she was surprised by how empty it was. Since she hadn't had a chance to go shopping earlier in the week, she decided to stop at a grocery store on her way home to pick up something for dinner. She was struck by the number of local businesses that were closed. When she finally found a deli that was open, the Asian woman behind the register seemed unusually compassionate. It made Chris want to say something, but she stopped.

When she got home, Chris decided to telephone the farm and say hello to everyone gathered for the reunion. They were all warm and expressed their support for her marathon effort. Everyone said they missed her, and she said the same. When she hung up the telephone, she felt nostalgic and self-pitying. She realized she hadn't felt that way about herself since she'd lost all the weight and graduated law school.

Chris took out her journal and began writing, making notes on all the things she wanted to achieve in her life, which goals she had reached, and which she had abandoned. She never wanted to be overweight again, but she also didn't want to spend another Thanksgiving alone. She realized it had been years since she'd sung in a chorus or choir, something she always loved. And she hadn't visited her college roommates since law school.

The next weekend, Chris drove out to visit her parents in the suburbs. She brought her running gear with her and went out for an hour's jog, but she didn't put in the miles she normally did on the weekend. The next week, she went to a chorus tryout during the evening, skipping her usual workout. She still exercised regularly in preparation for the marathon, but it no longer was the focus of her personal life. When one of the administrative assistants at the office asked if her goal was still finishing the marathon under 3:15, Chris said no: "Just finishing is okay."

"Today Is More Important Than Tomorrow"

Mike Everett knew he had the facts on his side when he sat with his wife to discuss funding their retirement plans. He'd gone online and downloaded articles describing how much they needed to save in order to maintain their current lifestyle once retired. Their broker had provided Mike with projections as well as suggested investments. Their accountant gave him some estimates of how much they'd save in taxes by maximizing their retirement contributions. Violet listened closely to all his arguments. But when she had a chance to respond, she asked him to forget about the numbers.

Violet reminded Mike that they had both chosen to move to the small city where they lived and to not have children so they'd have the money and freedom to travel and take risks in their careers. She was all for doing what they could to plan for the future, but she said that nothing was certain. "How much should we sacrifice our todays for our tomorrows?" she asked.

Mike confessed he hadn't thought of it in those terms. Sometimes he was so future focused and detail oriented, he forgot about the big picture and emotional issues. At the same time, he was afraid of not funding their retirement plans. "I always looked at it as paying ourselves first," he explained. "But I suppose we can pay ourselves with a trip, too."

He and Violet agreed to scale back both their retirement-funding plans and travel plans. They put half the maximum allowable contribution in their accounts, and rather than spending two weeks in Scotland, they went for one. While walking a trail in the Highlands, Mike turned to Violet and admitted, "You're right, sometimes today is more important than tomorrow."

"I Hope It's Enough"

Barbara, Chris, and Mike scaled back their aspirations and, in the process, improved their lives. They didn't give up their dreams, they just spread them across more of their lives. They may not have used the specific technique I've suggested, but they all came to the realization that their best was enough. You don't need to be the top-earning salesperson at your company, especially if it means missing your daughter's dance recital. You don't need to skip Thanksgiving in order to keep up your fitness program. You don't need to max out your retirement fund every year; there are times the money is better spent on a trip to the Highlands. You need to get to Scotland while you're still young enough to climb Ben Nevis. God doesn't reserve rewards for those who are the best; miracles come to those who do what they can. Miracles like being happy today.

In the early eighteenth century, the Hasidic movement was started by Rabbi Israel ben Eliezer. This famously holy man was eventually called the Baal Shem Tov, or Master of the Holy Name, because of the miracles that seemed to come from his prayers. Whenever he sensed the Jewish community in his native Ukraine was in danger, he would go to a special area in a nearby forest. He would ritually light a fire and then recite a special prayer. Miraculously, every time he did this, the danger would pass.

After the great rabbi's death, one of his disciples, Maggid of Mezritch, became leader of the community. One day he too sensed danger. He went to the same special area in the forest. "Master of the Universe," he prayed, "I am here in the holy spot, but I don't know the ritual of lighting the fire. I know I'm not the Baal Shem Tov, but I do know the special prayer. I hope it's enough." The rabbi said the prayer, and miraculously, the danger passed.

Years followed, and Rabbi Moshe Leib of Sasov, who succeeded Rabbi Maggid, again saw danger looming. As his predecessors did, he went to the special place in the forest and prayed: "Master of the Universe, I don't know how to light the ritual fire, and I don't know the special prayer, and I'm not the Baal Shem Tov, but I do know this is the holy spot. I hope it's enough." Once again, the peril was averted.

Later, the mantle of leadership settled on Rabbi Israel of Rizhin. Again, misfortune threatened the community. This time, the rabbi, sitting in his armchair, head in his hands, prayed to God: "Master of the Universe, I don't know how to light the ritual fire. I don't know the special prayer to recite. And I don't even know the holy place in the forest. I'm not the Baal Shem Tov. The best I can do is remember the rabbis who came before me and ask for your help. I hope it's enough." It was.

And it still is.

Your Best Is Enough

- Try to have everything and you'll end up with nothing.
  Contentment comes from having a well-rounded life.
- Because the baby boom generation was so large, and because
  our wealthy and powerful society catered to its needs and wants,
  boomers were raised to believe they could do and have anything.
  That belief has now spread throughout society.
- But even though the barriers to individual advancement and
  achievement have been broken down so you can achieve
  anything, you simply don't have enough time and/or money to
  have everything.
- That's okay, because a multifaceted life is more likely to provide
  fulfillment than a life devoted to only one pursuit.
- Rein in your dreams and expand their reach by exploring *all*
  your varied dreams and compromising so as to achieve as many
  of them in as many different aspects of your life as you can.
- Miracles, and happiness, come to those who do the best they can.

(8)

THE PAST IS PAST

A man is not old until regrets take the place of dreams.

—*John Barrymore*

There's no reset button for life. No matter how long you hold a grudge, regardless of how intricate and involved your plans for revenge are, you can never eliminate a past injury. Spend the rest of your life beating yourself up over a wrong choice you made or how you hurt a loved one, yet the error will never be changed and the hurt will never be undone.

That's why, for years, I've told people that anger and regret are impotent emotions. But now I realize they actually do have power: the power for self-injury and unhappiness. Hindsight isn't just 20/20, it's myopic and color-blind as well. Harboring anger and regret and agonizing over historic errors narrows your life to one of resentment and bitterness. And the longer you look backward, the fewer gray areas you'll see. Dwell on the past and events lose their reality and instead become extremes, either wonderful or terrible.

Hindsight isn't just 20/20, it's myopic and color-blind as well.

There's no more dramatic example of the impact of holding on to anger over past wrongs than Fay Weldon's novel *The Life and Loves of a She-Devil.*[*] Ruth, a tall, dark, powerfully built homemaker, is humiliated by her husband and his mistress, the slight, petite, blond novelist Mary Fisher. Ruth vows to get even. Ruth wants revenge, power, money, and "to be loved and not love in return." She dumps her admittedly ill-behaved children on her husband and launches into an extraordinary transformation that involves everything from ruthlessly manipulating others to undergoing life-threatening cosmetic surgery. Along the way to destroying her ex-husband and her rival, she transforms herself spiritually and physically into the person who hurt her. While there are many interpretations of the novel, mine is that Ruth, by trying to change her past, turns herself into a monster.

Understanding how destructive hindsight can be is helpful in leading a full life. But what's essential is realizing how empowering it can be to let the past go. Realizing the past is past, forgiving and apologizing, opens you to a wider, more joyous and fulfilling life. Forgiving the failings of others and accepting your own mistakes generates the kind of happiness and satisfaction of which most of us dream.

*Pantheon, 1984.

Forgiving the failings of others and accepting your own mistakes generates the kind of happiness and satisfaction of which most of us dream.

There's a wonderful moment in an otherwise mediocre movie that has always stayed with me. It sums up the attitude I think we should all adopt. The film is called *The Gumball Rally*,* and it's about an illegal cross-country road race of amateur sports car owners. The owner of a Ferrari hires a ringer, a professional racing car driver played by Raul Julia. Just before the race is about to start, the driver reaches up to the windshield and yanks off the rearview mirror. The owner of the car, sitting in the passenger seat, is stunned. "What are you doing?" he asks. The driver just smiles and says, "What's behind me doesn't matter."

Looking Back in Anger at Others

Most of us spend inordinate amounts of time looking in our lives' rearview mirrors. Sometimes it's a minor matter, like a Chicago Cubs fan dwelling over his team's century-long inability to win a World Series. But most times it's a weightier issue, such as siblings spending twenty years at each other's throats over who did and didn't do what when their father died.

Mitchell Betz, forty-six, hasn't had more than a few strained conversations with his older brother, Joshua, fifty, in almost three decades. Back when Mitch was in college and Josh was in law school, their father died from a sudden massive coronary. Mitch is a softhearted, compassionate person. His friends jokingly call him a "soft touch." Josh, while not estranged from the rest of the family, is somewhat cold and removed. When Mitch

*Directed by Charles Bail and written by Bail and Leon Capetanos.

arrived at his parents' home right after his father's death, he found his mother catatonic and his brother blasé. Rather than being emotionally and physically supportive of their mother, Josh was frosty. When he disagreed with one of his mother's decisions or ideas, he either argued or washed his hands of the subject. That left Mitch to handle most of the chores and arrangements. Josh returned to law school right after the funeral, leaving Mitch to deal with the aftermath. After helping his mother arrange the funeral, Mitch found himself spending months working with his mom on her finances. Whenever he asked Josh to pick up some of the slack, Josh said their mother needed to learn things on her own, and besides, he was too busy at law school. Ever since then, Mitch refused to have anything but the most cursory contacts with Josh, despite his mother's pleas for reconciliation.

Hindsight can infect more than just your personal life. Your feelings toward an employee can be forever colored by a single mistake.

When Joann Connors, thirty-nine, first hired Mary Gibbons, twenty-one, as her personal assistant, she was elated. An honors graduate of a prestigious university, the bubbly Mary impressed Joann during the interview process. Mary said she was looking for work as an assistant to a young, energetic attorney like Joann, since she was considering going to law school in the future. Mary's plan to get some real-world, related experience impressed Joann, an intense high achiever who valued pragmatism highly. But during her first few weeks on the job, Mary had trouble finding her stride. She seemed overwhelmed by the pace of the office and the need to juggle multiple tasks.

Arriving early on a Monday morning two weeks into Mary's tenure, Joann found an irate message on her voice mail. It seemed a valued client had left an urgent message on Thursday that was never returned. Despite Joann's pleas, explanations, and apologies, the client pulled his business. Joann contained her anger when confronting Mary later that day but made clear her disappointment and the need for the mistake never to be repeated.

During the next two years, it never was. In fact, Mary became the kind of efficient assistant Joann had at first hoped for. The problem was that Joann could never let go of that initial mistake. She never gave Mary more than minimal raises or mixed reviews. Finally, Mary gave notice that she'd taken a job with another law firm and would be going to law school at night.

Financial decisions that could dramatically impact your future financial life might be based on prior failings rather than current circumstances.

When Diane Manzetti, thirty-three, and her new husband, Bob, thirty-four, first started talking about buying a home, they knew they'd need to stretch their finances to the breaking point. One Sunday afternoon, the couple were having a relaxed brunch when the topic of conversation shifted to real estate. Bob offered to speak with his parents about possibly borrowing money to help with the down payment and asked Diane if she was willing to do the same. Diane's mood changed in a flash. Normally a relaxed and lighthearted person, she became curt and angry. When Bob pressed her to explain her change in temper, Diane started to cry and described her past financial dealings with her parents. Every time Diane had a goal or dream in mind that involved stretching her finances, her parents, particularly her father, immediately offered to help. When she was deciding which colleges to apply to, her father encouraged her to apply to Ivy League universities. He said he'd help out and that money shouldn't be an issue. But when she actually was accepted to Yale, her father developed cold feet and backed out. Unsure of how to pursue the issue on her own, the seventeen-year-old Diane went to a state college instead. Diane told Bob she refused to ask for financial help from anyone.

Regretting Our Past Actions or Inactions

Most often we look backward to incidents similar to those experienced by Mitch, Joann, and Diane. Someone else does something, or fails to do something, and as a result, we either experience pain or are harmed in some way. We're angry about what happened in the past, and no matter how much time passes, we lock that anger in place.

There are also times when, rather than being angry at someone else, we feel regret over our own past action or inaction. Admittedly, this kind of self-centered regret is rarer than outwardly directed anger. But when we do feel it, regret is even more harmful than anger. Let's face it, it's worse to beat yourself up than to be beaten up by someone else. You know your weak spots better than anyone, so when you take a swing at yourself, it's definitely going to do some damage. Like anger, regret can stem from incidents in your personal, financial, or work life.

You know your weak spots better than anyone, so when you take a swing at yourself, it's definitely going to do some damage.

Beth Kent, thirty-five, still feels bad about how long she strung along Ted Perry, thirty-six, her former fiancé. Beth and Ted dated in high school but then went their separate ways. When Beth returned to her hometown after graduating college, she reconnected with Ted, who had also returned home after school. Beth had had her heart broken in college by another boyfriend and was convinced she'd never find anyone again. When Ted came back into her life, eager to pick up where they'd left off, Beth didn't resist. Seeing her friends marrying and settling down, Beth believed Ted was her one and only chance. That was why she overlooked their obvious personality conflicts and dissimilar life goals. While she and Ted were busy making wedding plans, Beth found herself attracted to one of her co-workers, the forty-three-year-old Dave Kent, who seemed far more compatible than Ted. Dave obviously felt the same attraction. The day before the wedding invitations were to be mailed, Beth finally told Ted she couldn't marry him. He was understandably angry and, when he learned about Dave, suspected Beth of infidelity. Their split was bitter. Two years later, Beth married Dave. Despite knowing she did the right thing, Beth still regrets how she hurt Ted by restarting a relationship she knew wouldn't work and then dragging things out because of her fears and insecurities.

Tony Mancuso, fifty-one, regrets not sticking to his guns and following his instincts. After their divorce, Tony and his ex-wife split the proceeds from the sale of their suburban home. Tony took a new job teaching at a private university in a small city in a different state. While looking for a new place to live, he came across a very unusual property. The one-hundred-year-old Dutch Colonial was on a serpentine one-way road that snaked its way up a gorge. There were waterfall and woodland views from most of the windows. As the real estate broker noted, "Houses on this road don't come on the market often." The problem was, it was a bit more than he wanted to spend, and the house had some problems. While it was a five-bedroom, three-level house, the kitchen wasn't large enough to hold a full-size refrigerator. There were no full bathrooms; there were three showers and four toilets and sinks, but the showers were located in their own rooms, looking like closets from the outside. The seller, knowing the house was "unique," provided architectural plans for renovations that would create a more traditional floor plan. All Tony's instincts told him to grab this special home with its magnificent location. But he couldn't get over its unconventional elements, so he bought a small Victorian in the downtown area instead. While Tony's home has increased about 10 percent in value over the past ten years, the "unique" home he passed on sold five years ago for double its original price.

Allison Lee, thirty-one, regrets giving up on herself. After graduating from drama school, Allison moved to New York City and began doing stand-up comedy with an improv group while waiting on tables to pay her bills. Although she loved performing, Allison soon realized her strength was writing. She began churning out humorous columns and reviews for a number of "downtown" publications. Those pieces led to her being hired as a columnist for a fashion magazine that was trying to revitalize its image. The image makeover was a huge success, and Allison soon became a fixture in New York's hybrid publishing/fashion/media world. It was at a party after a gallery opening that Allison met a television producer who was looking for writers for a new sitcom. His idea was to build the show around a young single woman who was in the fashion business. Allison seemed a natural fit for the writing staff. Thrilled at the opportunity, Allison wrote a sample script and sent it along. The producer was bowled over. He loved her script and signed Allison to a contract. Her first couple of weeks on staff were a shock. No one had the time to train Allison or help her learn the ropes. She had been thrown into the deep end of the pool in the hope that she'd quickly teach herself to swim. Unfortunately, her first script didn't meet expectations. The producer, who stopped speaking to her directly, passed word through the head writer that the script was a disappointment and that she'd better make amends. With her back to the wall, Allison turned out another script. Although it was better than her first effort, the head writer candidly told her she was about to be let go. She had failed out of the box, and no amount of improvement was going to change the producer's opinion. With her meteoric rise turning into a meteoric fall, Allison fell into a depression. Her friends encouraged her to look for other script-writing work, but instead she returned to what was comfortable: magazine columns. Five years after her spectacular rise and fall, Allison still kicks herself for not getting right back on the horse.

Rejecting Victimhood

In all these cases, anger at others or regret over one's own actions or inactions becomes an obstacle to leading a fuller, happier life. "In history, as in human life," noted the Austrian writer Stefan Zweig, "regret does not bring back a lost moment and a thousand years will not recover something lost in a single hour." Mitch can hold his brother's behavior against him for the rest of his life and it won't relieve the emotional burden he carried all those years ago. In fact, by freezing the anger in place, Mitch ensures that the burden will weigh on him forever.

> Regret does not bring back a lost moment and a thousand years will not recover something lost in a single hour.
> —Stefan Zweig

When you dwell on past injuries, you perpetuate your pain. Keep living in the past and you don't allow a scab to develop and the wound to heal. Instead, you review the incident, over and over, and experience the pain, embarrassment, or guilt, over and over. Living in the past locks you into a psychological prison of victimhood.

Stop living in the past and you'll reject the image of yourself as a victim and embrace the image of yourself as an empowered individual. It's another of those spiritual ironies: once you stop trying to control your past and just let it go, you'll find the past no longer has control over you.

Once you stop trying to control your past and just let it go, you'll find the past no longer has control over you.

Glance, but Don't Stare

Don't get me wrong. I'm not suggesting you never reflect on the past or engage in postmortems of your actions or behaviors. The past is a wonderful teacher. We learn more from our mistakes than from our successes. Regressive analysis is, I believe, the best way to make all sorts of decisions. Considering whether to buy a home or not? Research how comparable properties have fared in recent years. Thinking about accepting a job with a different company? Investigate the company's human resources record and its past performance. Deciding whether or not to ask a co-worker out to dinner? Review how they've reacted to you whenever you've interacted. This kind of analysis makes sense. Hindsight becomes problematic when you stop visiting the past briefly and instead take up residence there. It's okay to glance backward, just don't stare.

There's also nothing wrong with looking backward in joy. Unfortunately, most of us look back to a negative rather than a positive past. Still, thinking of good things or times in the past can be wonderful because it actually leads us to think about the future. That's because positive feelings always give a sense that life is full of possibilities and opportunities. Think about your positive past and you'll end up looking forward to more of those experiences in the future. Remember good times and you'll believe there are more just ahead of you.

But once again, don't let remembrance turn into nostalgia. When you start dwelling in rather than visiting your past, even if it's a positive past, you end up hurting yourself. Extend your momentary reminiscence from a weekend visit to a weeklong stay and you'll lose the positive feelings about the future and will instead become melancholic. The longer you spend thinking about past good times, the more likely you are to generate complaints about the present. You might find yourself thinking back to how wonderful it was to spend Christmas at your grandparents' house when you were younger. Use that positive memory as the motivation to create an equally wonderful experience for your kids today rather than dwelling on it so long that your present pales in comparison.

Be aware that your past was neither as bad nor as good as you might think. We store memories using a kind of mental shorthand. Our brains simply don't have enough storage capacity to keep all the details of our past as well as our present. To save memory for our present, we edit incidents in our past down to their basic elements and categorize them: Your mother was loving and supportive. Your seventh-grade gym teacher was a bitter sadist. I'm not suggesting your mother was actually like Joan Crawford or your gym teacher was really an athletic Mr. Chips. It's just that, as human beings, they were complex creatures, neither entirely good nor completely bad. Glance backward and you'll be able to use these snapshots of people as tools for learning and improving your present. Stare at the snapshots and you'll begin filling in details, real or imagined, turning them into caricatures. In yet another irony, the more you dwell on the past, the less accurate your memories might be. Trust your mental shorthand to provide all the information needed for memories to serve as extraordinary educators.

Forgive, Don't Forget

To transform your past from a burden to a resource, you need to forgive those who have wronged you, yourself included. A court can't hold your past against you, and neither should you. You can't change what happened before. Forgiving the spouse who cheated on you doesn't mean what he or she did was right or that you condone the behavior. All it means is that you don't want to hold on to the anger.

I truly believe that, in general, people do the best they can. Sure, people may have let you down in the past, and others will probably let you down again in the future. But that's because they're human. You may not really know the full story behind their actions. The classmate who was cruel to you in high school may have been going home each day to abusive parents. That's not an excuse or a rationalization, it's just a fact. It doesn't make what they did acceptable, it just means there are things we don't know or understand and perhaps never will. I think it's best to realize there's a limit to our understanding and to forgive.

Make no mistake, there's a huge difference between forgiving and forgetting. To forgive doesn't mean to wipe the slate clean. It doesn't mean pretending the transgression never took place or forgoing any lessons the past might offer. "To forgive and forget means to throw away dearly bought experience," warned Arthur Schopenhauer. John F. Kennedy suggested, "Forgive your enemies, but never forget their names."

Forgiving means accepting that we are all flawed creatures, that no human being is perfect, and that we all make mistakes.

It's an act of acceptance, not of the other party's bad behavior, but of their humanity. It's a sign of wisdom. The psychiatrist Thomas Szasz wrote, "The stupid neither forgive nor forget; the naive forgive and forget; the wise forgive, but do not forget."

> The stupid neither forgive nor forget; the naive forgive and forget; the wise forgive, but do not forget.
>
> —Thomas Szasz

Forgiveness is a gift, but not in the way you might first think. It's not a gift for the person who transgressed against you, it's a gift for you. Forgiving allows you to put the past behind you. It lets you stop being a victim. Forgiveness is empowering.

I don't think there's a better example of the empowering nature of letting go than the story of two British mountain climbers, Joe Simpson and Simon Yates, described in Simpson's book *Touching The Void*.* The two climbing friends tackle a dangerous, ice-covered, twenty-one-thousand-foot peak in the Andes. On their descent, a blizzard hits. Joe falls off a ledge and suffers a broken leg. To get them both off the mountain alive, Simon attaches Joe to himself with a rope and begins slowly lowering him down. When the rope runs out, Joe secures himself to the mountain, Simon climbs down to meet him, and they repeat the process . . . over and over again.

After hours of this debilitating labor, at night, in white-out conditions, disaster strikes again. While being lowered, Joe suddenly falls into a crevasse. While Joe is hanging helpless, suspended in a giant ice cavern, Simon is hundreds of feet above, not knowing what has happened. Sitting on the mountainside, in the dark, in below-zero weather, Simon struggles to

*HarperCollins, 1989.

hold Joe. After hours of nearly superhuman effort, the weight and weather begin to take their toll. The frostbitten Simon feels himself sliding off the mountain. He's heard nothing from Joe and felt no sign of movement. Simon decides that Joe must be dead, and to keep himself from being pulled into the same chasm, he cuts the rope and struggles down the mountain alone.

Arriving at their tents, Simon is glad to be alive but filled with grief and guilt, thinking Joe is dead and that he's responsible. Unknown to Simon, when the rope is cut, Joe falls and lands on a ledge in the crevasse. Alive, but terribly injured and frostbitten, he begins to climb out. In an incredible feat of physical and spiritual stamina, Joe works his way out of the crevasse and then down the mountain. It takes him three days of crawling, but he arrives at their tent just as Simon is about to leave for civilization.

As their story becomes known, many people criticize Simon for cutting the rope and leaving Joe on the mountain, forgetting it was Simon who lowered Joe most of the way down. Few people had more reason to hold a grudge than Joe. And few people could have done something that could generate more regret than Simon. Yet Joe, realizing the past is past, forgave Simon, saying if he was in the same position, he probably would have done the same thing. Simon, also realizing the past is past, forgave himself for cutting the rope, knowing he had no choice. Both forgave, but neither forgot—how could they?—and each has grown spiritually stronger from the experience. They remain friends.

Learning to Let Go

I wish there were an easy, step-by-step process I could offer you so you could quickly forgive everyone who wronged you in the past; unfortunately, there isn't one. Ernest Kurtz, who has written extensively on forgiveness in his books on Alcoholics Anonymous, wrote that forgiveness doesn't come easily, but it does come suddenly. Citing psychological studies on forgiveness, he explained there is not a specific act of forgiving, but a sudden awareness that you've already forgiven. In other words, you're not aware of it until it has happened. "The harder you try to forgive," wrote Kurtz, "the harder it gets. Instead you just have to let it go. Stop trying to forgive and just let it go. Then at some point you'll realize you've forgiven. It results from openness less than effort." While I can't offer you a program for forgiving, I can offer you a couple of techniques to help cultivate a mind-set that's open to it happening. And you won't need to climb any mountains.

Take out your journal and turn to a fresh page. On top of the page write the word "Anger." Then try to list all the grudges you are holding. Don't worry about putting them in any kind of order, and include both large and small incidents. Angry at your mother for never having taught you to apply makeup? Write it down. Annoyed your wife ate the last two chocolate-chip cookies? List it. Leave a blank space after each entry. Once you've jotted down all those that come immediately to mind, focus on the first item. In the blank space after the first entry, write down exactly what you gain by holding the grudge. Having a hard time coming up with an answer? That's the point. Think about each entry and go through the same mental exercise. If in the future you remember further grudges, turn back to your journal, write them down, and try to come up with a benefit to holding on to your anger. Holding on to anger contributes nothing to your life.

Next, turn to another fresh page in your journal. Head the page "Regret." Write down as many incidents as you can in which you've wronged someone in one way or another. Again, these can be large or small, from your childhood or yesterday. Maybe you didn't empty the dishwasher Sunday morning because you were eager to get out the door and knew your wife would do it. Or perhaps you lied to your sister about already having plans for New Year's Eve because you didn't want to spend the holiday with her family. The person you wronged doesn't need to be aware of what you've done. For that matter, he or she doesn't even need to be alive. Once you've listed all the entries that come to mind right away, turn back to the first item. Now come up with a way to apologize for your action or inaction.

This might be a direct verbal apology. For instance, you could put down the journal, walk into the next room, and say, "Honey, I'm sorry I didn't empty the dishwasher on Sunday." If the person you wronged is dead, you can simply offer up a mental apology during a moment of meditation. Or, if it will help you heal, go to the person's grave or a place that held special meaning. If the other party isn't aware of having been wronged, like a sister who was lied to about holiday plans, don't spill the beans immediately. There are times when apologizing will do more harm to the other person. In those cases, you should engage in an act of compensation—for instance, inviting the sister and her family to stay at your home for a weekend.

Having apologized for all the items you've listed in your journal, try to make a practice of apologizing unhesitatingly for your actions whenever it's appropriate. What's the point of all this contrition? Well, first it's good for your soul. Publius Syrus wrote, "Confession of our faults is the next thing to innocency." But in this instance it has a further benefit. For years, whenever my wife, Corky, would point out something I'd done wrong, I'd try to rationalize my actions, or deny them, or launch a counterattack. Invariably we'd get into a fight. It took me only fifty years of marriage to figure out that if I just apologized, she'd forgive me right away and the whole incident would be behind us. I've realized that in almost every case, heartfelt apologies will be answered by forgiveness. And there's no better shortcut to forgiving others than being forgiven yourself. In cases where you don't apologize outwardly so as not to further hurt someone, the acts of contrition or compensation will help you forgive yourself. As Oscar Wilde once wrote, "It is the confession, not the priest, that gives us absolution."

"It Just Sort of Happened"

For years, Mitchell's estrangement from his brother, Joshua, hadn't really been a factor in his life. Whenever Mitchell was asked about it by friends, he explained there never really was a relationship between the two, so there was nothing to miss. But with the rift nearing its third decade, and with their mother's life nearing its eighth decade, things changed.

Mitchell and his wife, Cheryl, wanted to plan a party for his mother's seventieth birthday. The years hadn't changed Mitchell's feeling that Joshua let him down, nor, according to their mother's comments, had they changed Joshua's personality very much. But as he and Cheryl sat down to plan the party, Mitchell realized he had to somehow deal with his estrangement from Joshua.

Rather than take any overt action, Mitchell decided he'd delay dealing with the matter for as long as possible. For months, he and Cheryl made plans, prepared lists, and lined up vendors for the surprise birthday party. When it came time to send out invitations, they just included Joshua on the list with everyone else. Joshua sent an e-mail saying he'd be coming. As the date for the party neared, Mitchell got caught up in the last minute arrangements as well as finishing up a major project at work. The party went off without a hitch. Mitchell and Joshua exchanged pleasantries without incident.

Back at their hotel after the party, Cheryl asked Mitchell how he had gone about reconciling with Joshua. "I didn't really do anything," he explained. "To be honest, I kept putting it off and then it just sort of happened."

"I'm Going to Give Up My Anger"

After Diane told her husband, Bob, that she refused to ask anyone for financial help in buying a home, she avoided engaging in any further talk about it. Bob pushed her a couple of times, but she snapped at him and he backed down. The couple didn't stop house hunting, however.

Encouraged by their broker, Diane and Bob started to keep a house-hunting journal. They drew up lists of exactly what they wanted in a home: the breakdown and number of rooms, the style, the age, the condition, the neighborhood, and every other aspect of the house. They drafted checklists on what they wanted in a location. After meeting with their accountant, they started to keep daily lists of their cash spending and carefully outlined all their finances.

One Saturday afternoon, Diane and Bob sat down with their lists and notes and began analyzing how much they could spend on a home. On the advice of their accountant, they went over all their spending and looked for things to give up or ways to cut back in order to maximize the amount they could spend on a house. They determined that no matter how frugally they lived, they'd still come up short. Bob, without thinking and following the accountant's advice, suggested they next look at ways they could increase their income or savings. As soon as he saw the look on Diane's face, he realized he'd touched the raw nerve. He apologized.

Later that afternoon, while Bob was watching a football

game, Diane took out her house-hunting notebook and started looking at her list of "give-ups." She realized that while she was giving up so many little things that gave her pleasure—her daily Starbucks fix, going out for dinner once a week—there was something she could give up that would help them a great deal and that gave her pain rather than pleasure: her anger at her father. That evening, she told Bob she had no objection to his asking his family for help with a down payment: "I'm going to give up my anger."

"What Do I Have to Lose?"

After five years of writing magazine columns and articles, Allison felt burned out. Writing the same types of articles over and over was draining. In an effort to reenergize her writing and just have some fun, she began work on a romance novel, drawing on her own daydreams. Every evening and most weekends, she found herself drawn to the world she'd created in her "play novel." Allison told her friend Emily Wang about the book, and Emily insisted on reading it.

The day after giving Emily a copy of the manuscript, Allison received a gushing e-mail. Emily wrote that the book was great. "It's funny, it's tender, and it's sexy. I couldn't put it down. You were meant to do this."

Allison laughed it off at first and actually ignored the book for a couple of days. But on second thought, she decided to polish the book and send it off to an agent. Two weeks later, she received the manuscript back with a polite form rejection letter.

Crushed, Allison vowed to stick to her magazine writing. After wrapping the manuscript in a new envelope, she brought it to the closet in her spare bedroom, which she used for storage.

She tossed it into a box on the floor that contained her old scripts from the television show. Laughing and telling herself it was too clichéd a coincidence to use in a book or script, she went back to work on her next magazine article. But the coincidence stayed with her. Two weeks later, Allison dug the manuscript out of the closet and sent it off to another agent. She explained her change of heart to Emily: "What do I have to lose?"

Forgive and Forgive and Forgive

Mitchell, Diane, and Allison didn't use my techniques for fostering a mind that's open to forgiveness. Partly that's because I hadn't yet developed my techniques when they went through these situations. But primarily it's because there are as many paths to forgiveness as there are people who need to forgive and be forgiven. Forgiveness can come from denial, as it did for Mitchell. It can come from being faced with a stark choice, as was Diane. Or it can come from a coincidental epiphany like the one that struck Allison. Feel free to use my techniques. But don't rely on them alone. Just try to be open to forgiving. If you're open to it, the gift will come.

You have a choice. You can hold on to your anger and regret or you can let it go. There's an often told story of a conversation between two Holocaust survivors. When they meet once a year, Isaac and Natan talk for hours. As it inevitably must, the conversation turns to the horror they both shared. Isaac asks Natan, "Have you forgiven the Nazis?" After a moment's reflection, Natan answers, "Yes, I have." Isaac nods and then says, "Well, I haven't. I'm still consumed with hatred for them." Natan nods and then says, "In that case, they still have you locked in the camp."

You have a choice. You can hold on to your anger and regret or you can let it go.

The Jesuit author Dominic Maruca wrote that the memory of things past is like a worm that doesn't die. It can remain inside us and grow into a giant worm that keeps on gnawing away at our hearts, or it can be transformed into a beautiful butterfly and set free through the act of forgiveness.

This isn't something you can accomplish overnight; it takes time to let things go. There's no magic bullet to cure hindsight, no vaccine to ensure you'll never again look backward. From the day you resolve to get past your past, the process will be an ongoing part of your future. "Forgiveness is like faith," joked the aphorist Mason Cooley. "You have to keep reviving it." Speaking of faith, in the Bible, Peter asks Jesus how many times he has to forgive his brother if he keeps wronging him, suggesting seven times should be sufficient. Jesus responds by saying seven isn't nearly enough; instead Peter should plan on forgiving his brother seventy times seven times. In other words, there's no limit to how many times someone should be forgiven.

Epictetus wrote something similar. He believed that "human betterment is a gradual, two-steps-forward, one-step-back effort." He urged us to "forgive others for their misdeeds over and over and over again. This gesture fosters inner ease. Forgive yourself over and over and over again. Then try to do better next time."

The Past Is Past

- We spend inordinate amounts of time looking in life's rearview mirror.

- Most often it's because we're angry with someone else for something they did to us or failed to do for us.
- Sometimes it's because we regret something we did or something we didn't do.
- The past cannot be undone. Whatever the cause, looking backward does nothing but perpetuate your pain. It locks you into a prison of victimhood.
- It's okay to glance backward to learn, just don't stare.
- It's also okay to glance backward at happy times, just don't let it turn into nostalgia.
- To transform your past from a burden to a resource, you need to forgive others or yourself.
- Forgiveness comes only in time, but you can lay the foundation, realizing grudges are useless and apologizing for your own mistakes.
- Stop living in the past and you can embrace the image of yourself as an empowered individual.

(9)

TOMORROW IS TOO LATE

You don't save a pitcher for tomorrow. Tomorrow it may rain.

—*Leo Durocher*

Happiness is a state of mind, not a goal. The life you want is here, now, waiting for you to grab it. Too many of us spend our lives planning and hoping and dreaming about how wonderful life could be tomorrow if we got a promotion, met the right person, or inherited some money. We say that we'll be happy when we lose those stubborn thirty pounds, get our salary up to $100,000 a year, or pay off our mortgage. The poet Philip Larkin wrote, "Always too eager for the future, we / Pick up bad habits of expectancy. / Something is always approaching; every day / *Till then* we say . . ."

We act as if our happiness relies on other people, on fate, or on forces beyond our control. As a result, we fail to see how wonderful our lives are today. Pin your hopes on the future and you'll miss your chance. To paraphrase the songwriter Martin Charnin, tomorrow is always a day away.* Take responsibility for your own happiness and start living in the now. Tomorrow is too late. You can be happy today.

Take responsibility for your own happiness and start living in the now.

Of all the metaphysical things we need to deal with in our lives, I think time is the hardest on which to get a handle. Obviously, the past is that which has already occurred. But that's both something that happened thirty years ago and something that happened thirty seconds ago. Your high school prom is in the past, but so is the sentence you've just completed reading. The future, clearly, is that which hasn't yet occurred. But again, that's something likely to happen ten minutes from now and something else you hope happens ten centuries from now. Your plans for dinner are in the future, but so is the next ice age. This makes the present, the time in which we are actually living, a simultaneously abstract and very narrow concept. The architect Frank Lloyd Wright called the present "the ever moving shadow that divides yesterday from tomorrow." The poet Thomas Moore wrote of it as "this narrow isthmus 'twixt two boundless seas / The past, the future,—two eternities!" And the philosopher Marcus Aurelius warned: "Remember that man's life lies all within this present, as 't were but a hair's-breadth of time; as for the rest, the past is gone, the future yet unseen. Short, therefore, is man's life, and narrow is the corner of the earth wherein he dwells."

---

*"Tomorrow, you're always a day away" is the actual line from the song "Tomorrow," which he wrote for the Broadway musical *Annie*.

What's amazing is that this shadow, this narrow isthmus, this hair's-breadth of time, has the possibility of providing all the joy and contentment we need. That's because the present isn't so much a space in time as it is a state of mind.

You're a Human Being, Not a Human Becoming

When you look at the present in terms of time, it becomes an infinitesimal thing. If the past is everything that has already happened, and the future is everything that hasn't yet happened, all that's left for the present is the briefest of moments, so brief it's almost impossible to discern. "We are like men standing on a narrow footbridge over a railway," wrote the novelist Samuel Butler. "We can watch the future hurrying like an express train toward us, and then hurrying into the past, but in the narrow strip of present we cannot see it. Strange that that which is most essential to our consciousness should be exactly that of which we are least definitely conscious." Your present is like that rushing train, a total blur. Unable to get a handle on, let alone live in, this kind of blurry present, you pin your hopes on the future. It actually seems quite practical. After all, the future seems to stretch out before us almost infinitely. It seems to give us plenty of time in which to land new jobs, meet life mates, or learn the guitar. It's easy to believe your hopes and dreams and goals can all be answered tomorrow.

But this is just an optical illusion. It may look clear and inviting, but it never actually arrives; it remains all potential and no reality. When you look to the future for your happiness, you guarantee you'll never be happy. Leaving things to tomorrow is a self-perpetuating process. You will always have more tomorrows until your last day of life, and if you believe in an afterlife or reincarnation, you'll have tomorrows even after your death. If you look to the future for your happiness, you will indeed always have the possibility of achieving contentment . . . but you'll never actually get there. It's as if you're on a voyage looking for the edge of the earth. You keep traveling, thinking the edge of the earth is right there at the horizon line. But no matter how long you travel, how far you go, you never actually get there. Your goal is always visible but always out of reach. Live your life this way, rely on the future for your happiness, and you're a human becoming, not a human being.

If you look to the future for your happiness, you will indeed always have the possibility of achieving contentment . . . but you'll never actually get there.

Don't look at the present as a brief moment, a slice of time between the past and the future; view it as an experience, as a state of mind. The past is what you were, and as I wrote in the previous chapter, it's past. If you're stuck there, you're remembering, not living. The future is what you might be, it's purely conditional and entirely uncertain. Focus on the future and you'll always be hoping, never really living. The present, on the other hand, is what you are; it's not what you were or what you might be. The present is the experience of living, not remembering or hoping. Let's say you're sitting in a theater, watching a great movie or a terrific play, or perhaps you're in a concert hall, listening to a wonderful performance. You're not thinking of the drive home or what you'll be having for dinner afterward, you're in the moment. Bring that approach to your life and you'll achieve contentment. Ralph Waldo Emerson wrote that man "cannot be happy and strong until he too lives with nature in the present, above time."

The present is the experience of living, not remembering or hoping.

Plan for It, Just Don't Live There

As I've written before, I'm not saying you shouldn't plan for tomorrow. Short-term and even long-term planning is, in fact, prudent. It's something I've tried to promote for as long as I've been consulting and writing. And I believe prudent planning includes deciding when to start a family as much as calculating when to ask for a raise or determining how much to save and invest for when you get older and your earned income drops. But there's a big difference between planning for the future and living in it.

Planning for the future means acknowledging certain things are inevitable and require forethought and, perhaps, some preparatory actions. For instance, as much as we'd like to deny or ignore it, we are mortals. Depending on the circumstances of your life, that acknowledgment could prudently require as little as writing a simple will and naming an executor or as much as buying sufficient life insurance to pay for the temporary support of a spouse and the education of a couple of children. I also think it's savvy planning to set aside enough money to pay for extraordinary bills you know are coming, like taxes. And I believe it makes sense to plan on having to get another job at some point, since there's no such thing anymore as lifelong employment.

Living in the future means counting on it to provide or be the environment that offers you the happiness or satisfaction you currently lack. It's not that you're counting on one particular event happening—it's that you expect there to be wholesale change in your life in the future, moving you from discontent-ment to contentment.

"Someday I'm Going to Be a Successful Musician"

Living in the future means telling yourself you're going to be-come a happy and successful jazz pianist in the future rather than the unhappy junior high school music teacher you are to-day. That's what Cynthia Hernandez tells herself.

Cynthia, thirty-nine, has always loved music. She began tak-ing piano lessons when she was only eight years old, and as she jokes to her friends, "I've just never stopped." Cynthia grew up in a solidly middle-class family. Her father was a midlevel ex-ecutive in an auto parts supply company. Her mother was a school nurse. While Cynthia and her younger sister Miranda were all encouraged to pursue creative interests as well as their schoolwork, she was the only one to stick with it. She had an opportunity to attend a performing arts high school, but her father thought she shouldn't put all her eggs in one basket. That philosophy continued through her college years at a state university, where Cynthia took a dual major in music and edu-cation.

Once she graduated, Cynthia gave some thought to taking a waitressing job or some other noncareer position and trying to break into the music business. Her parents once again encour-aged her to play it safe. Cynthia remembers talking to her par-ents about sharing an apartment in a particular part of the city and her mother's jaw dropping: "That's where my parents lived when they first came to this country. We didn't work hard to send you to college so you could move back to the barrio." Al-though Cynthia was upset for a few months, she soon realized the bohemian life wasn't right for her. A stylish dresser whose makeup and hair are always perfect, Cynthia admits to having a weakness for shoes and handbags.

Rather than concentrating on her music, Cynthia took a job teaching at a junior high school near the suburb where she grew up. Young and enthusiastic, she became popular with the students and with her peers. After only a couple of years, she also became director of the choir and jazz band. As her income climbed, her lifestyle improved. Once she earned tenure and felt secure, Cynthia bought a condo apartment large enough to hold the baby grand piano she'd always dreamed of owning.

Even though she's now a proficient teacher and a fixture in her school, Cynthia continues to take lessons and work on her own music. She takes jobs playing at weddings and has a regular monthly gig at a nightclub owned by a family friend. While still single, Cynthia has an active and interesting social life combining co-workers from school and friends she's met through her music.

Still, Cynthia frequently speaks to her family and close friends about how depressed and unhappy she is with her life. "I feel like I'm still struggling to get to where I want to be," she told her sister Miranda one recent weekend. "Someday I'm going to be a successful musician."

"Things Will Be Different When I Make It Big"

Living in the future means telling yourself you're going to be a satisfied affluent financial planner in the future rather than the forlorn tax adviser you are today. That's what Keith Boyd, forty-three, tells himself.

The son of a single mother who worked as an aide in a nursing home, Keith always tried to outwork everyone else around him. An excellent student at the inner-city high school he attended, Keith decided to pursue a career in accounting since it seemed to offer him the quickest route to being a professional. Growing up watching his mother work for less than paternal employers, and having put in time of his own working at dead-end jobs, Keith wanted never to have to rely on a boss to put food on his family's table. Using subsidized student loans and grants, he was able to attend a small but elite private college. There he majored in both accounting and finance. Recruited to join a number of large accounting firms before he even graduated, Keith took the highest paying of the offers. He barely had time to hang up his graduation gown before he was on the job at the firm's main midwestern office.

While there, Keith met his future wife, Jocelyn, who worked as a receptionist. After four years he was made partner, and, feeling secure, they got married. Keith and Jocelyn bought a small home in an older, inner-ring suburb. It wasn't as large a home or in as prestigious an area as Keith wanted, but it made sense financially. Though he preferred investment planning, Keith specialized in tax work because he thought that would provide him with the most secure practice. After another five years at the firm, Keith had built a good reputation and a stable of loyal clients. He and Jocelyn had two sons. It was very important to Keith that his sons grow up with a parent at home, so Jocelyn gave up her job. That meant they didn't live as luxuriously as some of their peers who had two incomes, but both thought it was worth the sacrifice.

As the years went by, Keith's career remained solid. His practice and his role in the firm grew, and so did his sons. Rather than go on European vacations, he and Jocelyn took domestic trips with the kids. Instead of redoing the kitchen, they sent the kids to summer camps. The college funds took money that might have gone for a new car. Whenever he'd gripe about things at work, Jocelyn would suggest he finally leave the firm and start his own investment-counseling practice. But Keith never felt comfortable taking the risk.

Around the time of his forty-fifth birthday, Jocelyn noticed Keith seemed depressed. Never an outgoing person, he was growing more withdrawn, almost sullen. Whenever she'd try to engage him in conversation, he'd cut her short. Finally, one night when they were having dinner out, she got him to open up. "I'm not unhappy with us," he stressed, "it's just that I feel like I'm always settling for less. I know things will be different when I make it big."

"We'll Be Fine When Things Finally Settle Down"

Living in the future means telling yourself your marriage will be wonderful in the future, after the kids have left home, rather than tense and difficult, which is what it is now. That's what Candace Kellog told herself.

Candace, thirty-one, and her husband, Earl, also thirty-one, were high school sweethearts. Earl went away to college, and Candace stayed in their Northern California hometown to go to the local community college. That led to a short-lived breakup, but within six months they were back together to stay. After Earl graduated, he got a job at a software company not far from their hometown. Candace took a job managing a woman's clothing store. To their friends, Candace and Earl were the epitome of opposites attracting. Candace is funny and chatty. A petite redhead, she has always been the one to lighten up a party. A lover of music and art, she loves spending time at galleries and concerts. Earl, on the other hand, is quiet and private. A tall blond, he can be intense and serious, especially when discussing cars and computers, his two hobbies. When part of the large social group in their hometown, their differences seemed exciting rather than divisive. But when they moved to a town nearer

Earl's office and had only each other for company, conflicts developed.

Candace was eager to go out and meet people and suggested taking in various gallery shows and performances. Earl, happy to stay at home and uncomfortable meeting new people, wasn't interested. When Candace started taking classes and going out on her own, Earl became jealous. Their relationship wasn't going as well as Candace wished, but when she found out she was pregnant, her qualms vanished. She told her mother that once they had their baby, they'd be drawn back together. And for the first three years of their daughter Terri's life, they were.

As the baby grew and their rental apartment seemed to shrink, Candace and Earl started getting on each other's nerves again. Whenever he had free time, Earl preferred working on his car or going online to playing with Terri. He rarely and then only begrudgingly took charge of Terri so Candace could have some time to herself. Candace felt that if only they had a home of their own, things would be different. They'd have more room and wouldn't be "in each other's faces all the time." With the help of both sets of parents, Candace and Earl bought a charming three-bedroom ranch just before their daughter was due to start kindergarten.

Once Terri started school, Candace went back to work part-time. The money was helpful, but more valuable to Candace was the chance to get out of the house and create a new social network. Their handful of friends were mostly co-workers of Earl's and their wives. Terri is her mother's daughter. An active, highly social child, she loves dancing, singing, and gymnastics. Candace jokes that she wishes she had as busy a social schedule as her daughter. Earl received a promotion and was working longer hours than ever before. The time pressures impacting all three led to some sparks. Whenever Candace asked Earl not to work so late and to get more involved in Terri's afterschool activities, his response was to note that it was his overtime pay that was paying for those activities. On a visit to her mother's, Candace vented some of her frustrations but quickly added, "We'll be fine when things finally settle down."

The Future Is Unknowable

One problem facing Cynthia, Keith, and Candace is that if they continue to look to the future, they'll never be happy. Partly that's because if you're viewing the present and future in terms of time, the future never actually arrives. But another problem is less abstract than practical: The future isn't predictable. You don't know what's going to happen.

No amount of study and insight will allow you to accurately predict the future. As the playwright Eugène Ionesco wrote, "You can only predict things after they have happened." The novelist Angela Carter wrote, "To pin your hope upon the future is to consign those hopes to a hypothesis, which is to say, a nothingness. Here and now is what we must contend with."

> To pin your hope upon the future is to consign those hopes to a hypothesis, which is to say, a nothingness. Here and now is what we must contend with.
>
> —Angela Carter

Let's say you put off starting your own office-cleaning business until you have less personal debt. You assume you'll continue to pay off your credit cards, mortgage, and your oldest son's college loans, so "in the future" you'll be better able to borrow for the business. You assume everything will happen according to your mental plan. In his wonderful book *The Devil's*

Dictionary, Ambrose Bierce defined the future as "that period of time in which our affairs prosper, our friends are true and our happiness is assured."

Unfortunately, that's not always how things turn out. Perhaps on the way to work a deer runs in front of your car, and you swerve to avoid it and hit a tree. You're fine, but you need to have repairs and bodywork done to your car. It's not going to bankrupt you, but since you don't have the cash and you need to have a car to get to work, you pay for the repairs with your credit card. Eight months later, your refrigerator gives up the ghost. A year after that, your younger son is accepted into a program that will let him study in France for a semester. Then your twenty-fifth wedding anniversary rolls around and you know it would make your wife's year if you buy her those diamond earrings you passed over last Christmas. "Predictions of the future," wrote Hannah Arendt, "are never anything but projections of present automatic processes and procedures, that is, of occurrences that are likely to come to pass if men do not act and if nothing unexpected happens; every action, for better or worse, and every accident necessarily destroys the whole pattern in whose frame the prediction moves and where it finds its evidence."

While you're making plans to be happy in the future, things happen, good and bad. Life doesn't stand still just because you've made a mental calculation freezing it in place. And it's not just your own situation that factors in. Interest rates could go up, making it harder to make your loan payments. War in the Middle East could send gas prices through the roof. A new widget could be invented in a plant in Argentina that hurts the business of your area's major employer, which closes three of its plants, which lowers the demand for office-cleaning services, making the business less profitable. The apocryphal butterfly that flaps its wings and starts a storm system could just as easily and dramatically change your life as well as the climate. "The future is inevitable and precise," wrote the novelist Jorge Luis Borges, "but it may not occur. God lurks in the gaps."

Only God knows what the future holds, so your counting on it to provide the environment that will finally make you happy isn't just foolish, it's presumptuous. Stop writing the script for tomorrow. Today isn't a dress rehearsal, it's your life.

Today isn't a dress rehearsal, it's your life.

The Only Thing You Lack Is Gratitude

How do you stop living in the future? Realize the only thing you lack in the present is gratitude. I know, I'm sure there are things missing in your life. Maybe you don't have a life partner, or you're out of work, or your child is ill. But you still have things to be grateful for. If nothing else, be grateful you're alive. It's safe to assume the alternative isn't fun.

The people who seem most able to live in the present are those who have come face-to-face with their own mortality. Having come through a life-threatening situation, they look on every subsequent day of life as a wonderful gift. That's what happened to me.

In 1978, I was the forty-eight-year-old chairman of an American Stock Exchange–listed venture capital firm. I had a lovely wife, Corky, and four incredible children, Michael, Lori, Tracy, and Dana. We had recently moved from a big home on suburban Long Island to a twelve-room apartment on New York's Park Avenue. During the summer, the whole family stayed at a house we'd built on Martha's Vineyard. Was I happy? No. I was living in the future. Not only couldn't I stop and smell the roses, I couldn't stop and smell dinner on the table, since I didn't get home until 10:00 p.m. I was smoking three packs of cigarettes a day, and my only workout was bending my elbow. As part of my unending climb up Mount Olympus, I took a job as the real estate specialist for an international bank headquartered on Wall Street. After a brief time on the job, I started feeling under the weather. After a month of prevarication and procrastination, I finally went to see our family doctor, Dr. Dove. He heard my smoker's cough and listened to my labored breathing and immediately ordered a chest X-ray. Two days later, Dr. Dove called to say they'd found a troubling black spot on my lung. He gave me a tuberculosis test, which came back negative, and scheduled a follow-up X-ray. Meanwhile he set up consultations for me with cancer specialists. The oncologist and the surgeon wanted to schedule surgery right away, but Dr. Dove pushed for a biopsy of the spot.

While we were waiting for the biopsy results, Corky and I went through all the obstacles we faced to keep the family afloat. There were mortgages, tuitions, and medical bills. I knew I'd be out of work, perhaps forever, and we couldn't get by on the salary Corky was making from her secretarial job. Things looked grim, to put it mildly. Then Dr. Dove came into the hospital room and said, "Congratulations, you have tuberculosis." At that moment, my life turned around.

I was given a reprieve. I felt that every day from that point on was a gift from God, sent via Dr. Dove. All the material things Corky and I figured out we stood to lose meant nothing. When we were going over the list, I had thought to myself, I'd give them all up to spend another day with my wife and children. Now here I was, told I would have that day and many more to follow. I wasn't changed so much that I turned around and sold everything. We still have the apartment and the summer house and, truth be told, more. But I've stopped living in the future.

I'm grateful for everything I have and covet nothing other than more years with my family. I realized that what I lacked for those first forty-eight years of life was gratitude for what I already had. I didn't appreciate that every day is a priceless gift. I didn't understand that tomorrow was too late.

It has been almost thirty years since my life turned around. In that time, the immediacy of the lesson I learned faded a bit. I think that's only natural. Maybe because I tell the story quite often to inspire others, it lost some of its power for me. But life has a way of providing refresher courses. As I wrote earlier in the book, in the past five years I lost my mother, younger brother, younger sister, and father, all after prolonged illnesses. It's hard to accept that anything good comes from death, but the losses of these beloved people have ironically given me renewed opportunities to be grateful for what I do have.

Taking Inventory

Going through experiences like these can help you move from living in the future to living in the present. But as much as I value the insight I've gained, I don't recommend the processes I went through to earn them. Thankfully, you can work toward the same awareness with a lot less pain. All you need to do is take inventory.

Take out your journal and turn to a fresh page. On top of the page write the heading "Things for Which I'm Grateful." Start by writing, "I'm alive," and move on from there, line by line, filling as many pages as you need.

Start by concentrating on those you love. Write about family and friends and pets from your past and present. For instance, you might write, "I'm grateful for my friendship with Nelson Barber, who always makes me laugh." Don't forget to include groups of people as well. Maybe you're a New York Rangers fan who's grateful for the 1994 team that finally won the Stanley Cup. Or perhaps you're a music lover who's grateful for the Talking Heads.

Next, move on to places you love or loved. The list could include special spots that have always brought you serenity, or it could consist solely of your home. You might write something like "I'm grateful for our apartment overlooking the harbor." It might also consist of places you've been to only once—say, the little pension in Vienna where you spent a magical weekend with your spouse, or the summit of Mount Rainier, which you climbed with your brother last summer.

Turn to things you value. I know, people are always railing against materialism. But let's be real: there are things that give us joy. It could be your library, or a set of golf clubs, or your collection of shoes. No one is going to read this list, so don't feel self-conscious about offering thanks for some inanimate objects others might think valueless. If you're grateful for your Weber grill or your string of pearls, there's nothing wrong with acknowledging it.

I know it could feel a bit corny to sit there compiling lists of things for which you're grateful. But I think most of us have grown too cynical about our lives. We've stopped appreciating what we have. That's one of the reasons we tend to live in the future. We look for the flaws in everything, whether it's a public figure or ourselves. Our culture has become fixated on improvements, whether it's to our home, our relationships, or our bodies. The message that's coming across is that things will be better if you lose some weight, or redecorate your apartment, or have some prima donna choose your new wardrobe and hairstyle. In other words, you'll be happy in the future. Well, take it from me, you have everything you need right now to be happy. In fact, you've more than you need.

Making a list of things for which you're grateful is nowhere near as dramatic as facing your mortality. I don't for a minute think this simple exercise is going to provide you with the kind of instant epiphany experienced by those who confront their own deaths. But that's okay. This isn't magic. There's no single incantation or prayer that's going to instantly change your attitude toward life. This is a process. You're going to have to work at living in the present, at being happy. On days when you're feeling down, turn back to the list you've compiled and reread what you've written. Then, after a few minutes' reflection, add some new entries to the list. You'll find that whenever you spend time looking for reasons why your life right now is good, you end up finding them.

Another way to make yourself feel better is to tell people you're grateful for what they've done for you. This needn't be formal or part of a ritualized thanksgiving. Instead, when an opportunity arises, just thank people for coming into your life. Let's say you're sitting at a coffee shop after work, sharing a good laugh with a friend. Just turn to her and say something like "I have a great time with you, thanks for being my friend." That's not so hard, is it? But believe me, such a little gesture will mean a lot to the other person, and that will make you feel great.

"I'm a Successful Person"

Cynthia Hernandez knew something was wrong the minute the principal of her school appeared in the doorway of her classroom. After calling Cynthia outside, he explained he'd received a telephone call saying her father was dead from a sudden and massive coronary.

Throughout the process of planning and getting through the funeral, Cynthia and her sister Miranda kept their emotions under control, partly because there was so much to do and partly because they had to be strong for their mother. Finally, on the day after the funeral when the two sisters were cleaning up while their mother took a nap, Cynthia broke down. She tearfully told Miranda that she felt terrible her father hadn't seen her become successful. "He'd worked so hard for us, and I couldn't make him proud," she confessed.

Miranda listened, then closed her eyes for a moment. "What the hell are you talking about?" she snapped. "You've got a great job, a nice apartment, you're out all the time, and you travel all the time. Daddy thought you were great. You're the one who was disappointed."

Shocked by the response, Cynthia didn't know what to say, so she just dropped it.

Later that week, Cynthia went to church on her lunch hour. She said a quick prayer for her father, then decided to sit for a time and meditate. To her surprise, Miranda's words came back to her. For the next few days, Cynthia began taking an informal inventory of her life. She knew she was a very good teacher, and the kids seemed to love her. She'd just had her apartment repainted and had bought a new couch and love seat for the living room. She had started dating a guy, a guitarist she'd met at a wedding gig. She and two of her friends were planning a trip to Paris in the fall.

That weekend, she and her sister were having dinner at their mother's house. When their mother left the room to take a telephone call, Cynthia opened up to Miranda. She thanked her for what she'd said and told Miranda she'd given it a lot of thought. "You were right," she admitted. "I was so wrapped up in what I've always wanted to happen, I couldn't see what I already had. I'm a successful person."

"I've Made It Already"

When Keith Boyd finally opened up to his wife, Jocelyn, about the reason for his being depressed, she took his hands in hers. Plaintively, she told him he owed it to himself and the rest of the family to go see someone about what he was feeling. Never one for psychotherapy, Keith started to object, but Jocelyn cut him short. She suggested he speak to a friend of theirs, a successful career counselor who had started off as a therapist. "You've always said he's great, and you've sent lots of clients to speak with him, so why don't you try it?"

After the first few moments of his first session with the counselor, Keith knew Jocelyn had been right. Instead of doing some kind of psychological probing of his childhood, the counselor took him through a pragmatic process of self-assessment. Keith drew up lists of what he liked and didn't like about his job and his life. He wrote down what he thought were his strengths and what he believed were his weaknesses. The counselor had Keith draft a new résumé, putting all his professional accomplishments down on paper. Then the counselor asked Keith to create a personal résumé as well.

Keith had begun the process believing he'd end up with a new plan for his future. He thought he'd uncover what he needed to do with his career and life in the future to make him happy. After six sessions with the counselor, he announced that he'd figured some things out.

Jocelyn was surprised when Keith came home early from his counseling session. She rarely asked him what was discussed, but this time she couldn't resist. He smiled and explained that he'd spent six weeks figuring out that he had a great life right now. Sure, they'd made sacrifices, and things weren't always perfect at work, but he'd realized he was where he wanted to be. "I don't know what I was thinking," he admitted. "I've made it already."

"Things Are Still Crazy, but We're Fine Now"

Despite the placating words to her mother after venting her frustrations, Candace Kellog wasn't sure things would be fine for her family. The tension between Candace and her husband, Earl, was frightening her, and she was afraid it might be having an impact on their daughter, Terri. What was more frightening to her, however, was how readily Earl agreed to go speak with their minister. It was just an indication to her of how bad things really were.

Candace and Earl's minister began by encouraging them both to open up and be honest about their anger and frustration with each other and to be more accommodating. Venting their feelings had an almost immediate effect, and the tension around the house eased. Candace worked hard at expressing her appreciation for how hard Earl was working and being supportive of his finding ways to release some of his work frustrations. Earl did his best to be more understanding of Candace's need to socialize and made a concerted effort to take a more active role in Terri's activities.

At a subsequent meeting, their minister said something that struck a chord with Candace. The minister said she wasn't surprised by some of what was happening between them. After all, she noted, Candace and Earl had gotten together when they were very young. The minister sensed that the couple had an idealized view of what married life would be like and, as a result, were disappointed in their present. She asked Candace and Earl to talk about all the things that were good about their lives now. Candace, struck by how much she'd been overlooking the positive aspects of her present life, followed up the session by making lists of all the things in her entire life, not just her marriage, for which she was grateful.

A few weeks later, Candace took a drive to visit her mother while Earl took Terri to a local museum for the day. After lunch, Candace's mother couldn't resist asking about the sessions with the minister. Without going into too much detail, Candace eased her mother's fears. "Things are still crazy," she explained, "but we're fine now."

Reach Out to Sounding Boards

Cynthia, Keith, and Candace all needed someone else to help them realize they were living in the future instead of the present. I think that's the case for most of us. Unless you go through some kind of traumatic event, it's hard to come to this realization on your own. I hope this chapter, and actually this entire book, has in some small way served that role for you. I encourage you to reach out to others if you think it will help, whether they're family, friends, clergy or therapists. Obviously, I can't reach out to each one of you and address the circumstances of your life in such a specific way that it immediately rings true and has an impact. I've tried as best I can within the confines of the written word. And I'll be happy to do more if you'd like. As I've written in many of my other books, I'll readily respond to any e-mails or letters sent to me via the publisher of this book. I've met and spoken with many readers in the past this way, and they've all enriched not just my work, but my life.

I make this offer not out of some effort to ingratiate myself with you. Obviously, since you've already gotten this far into this book, you've found what I've written helpful. I make this offer because I feel so strongly about the message that tomorrow is too late. If you take away only one thing from this book, I hope it's the realization that happiness doesn't come from tomorrow, it comes from today. Your life is what's happening right now.

Happiness doesn't come from tomorrow, it comes from today. Your life is what's happening right now.

Return to the Joy of Childhood

The poet Alastair Reid addressed this so well that I'd like to quote him at some length. He wrote, "The principal difference between childhood and the stages of life into which it invariably dissolves is that as children we occupy a limitless present. The past has scarcely room to exist, since, if it means anything at all, it means only the previous day. Similarly, the future is in abeyance; we are not meant to do anything at all until we reach a suitable size. Correspondingly, the present is enormous, mainly because it is all there is. . . . Children have an infinite power to transform; they are able to make the world into anything they wish, and they do so, with alacrity. . . . Later in life, the transformations are forbidden; they may prove dangerous. By then, we move into a context of expectations and precedents of past and future, and the present, whenever we manage to catch it and realize it, is a shifting, elusive question mark, not altogether comfortable, an oddness that the scheme of our lives does not allow us to indulge. Habit takes over, and days tend to slip into pigeonholes, accounted for because everything has happened before, because we know by then that life is long and has to be intelligently endured."

Life shouldn't be something to be endured until the future arrives. Your present should be thrilling, exhilarating, and inspiring. And it can be if you embrace it. My wish for you is that you're able to somehow get back to the joy you experienced as a child. As far as I can tell, we all get only one chance at this. We might as well enjoy ourselves while we're here. Sure, there's pain and sorrow in life. But there's also exhilaration and joy. You can't avoid the pain and sorrow. So don't defer the exhilaration and joy until some nonexistent tomorrow. Let yourself be happy now.

Tomorrow Is Too Late

- Too many of us spend our lives planning and hoping and dreaming about how wonderful our lives could be in the future. As a result, we fail to see how wonderful life is today.
- Take responsibility for your own happiness and start living in the now. Tomorrow is too late. You can be happy today.
- When you look at the present in terms of time, it becomes infinitesimal and blurry. Instead, look at the present as an experience, as a state of mind.
- The present is the experience of living, not remembering or hoping.
- Prudent planning is fine, but there's a big difference between planning for the future and living in it.
- Take inventory of all the things for which you're grateful: the people you love, the places you enjoy, the things that bring you pleasure.
- Don't defer happiness to some nonexistent tomorrow. Let yourself be happy today.

(10)

OUT OF YOUR MIND

A thought which does not result in an action is nothing much, and an action which does not proceed from a thought is nothing at all.
—*George Beranos*

Y ou know how to be happy. Having read this far, you realize happiness won't come from getting a new job, finding a mate, losing weight, buying a home, having a child, changing location, getting a new car, buying a plasma TV, or going back to college. You realize that even if you won the lottery tomorrow, you could still be unhappy. Happiness comes from internal, not external, factors. The eight essential secrets to leading a life without regret are all in your head. I didn't plant them. They were there all along. All I've done in this book is shine a light on them and perhaps dust them off a bit for you. Everything you need to be happy was and is in your mind. Now you need to get it out of your mind and into the real world.

Early in this book, I wrote about how having the secrets to

happiness in your head is a mixed blessing. It means each and every one of us has the potential to be happy, regardless of external circumstances. It doesn't matter whether you're in a relationship or single, fit or out of shape, wealthy or poor, gainfully employed or out of work. You have the power to be happy. But it also means *only* you have the power to make you happy. Your happiness is your own responsibility. It's time to be accountable.

That's no small task. It's very tempting to blame others or outside factors for our unhappiness. God knows you've probably had your share of hardships and bad luck throughout your life. We all have.

Perhaps you had a parent who, intentionally or unknowingly, left your self-esteem in tatters. Jimmy Mitchell, forty-six, has struggled with his weight, and as a result, his self-image, for his entire life. His mother grew up in Nazi-occupied Europe and experienced real hunger. As a result, she became somewhat obsessed with providing her children with enough food. Then her husband died early from a heart attack, which she blamed on her cooking. As a result, she had a love/hate relationship with food, which she passed on to Jimmy.

Maybe there was someone whose offhanded criticism left a scar that's never healed. Rachel Levy, thirty-five, still refuses to go to the beach or the pool because she'd have to put on a bathing suit. When she was at a pool party in junior high school, the teacher supervising the outing commented on her "thunder thighs," and the whole group of kids joined in the laughter.

Or maybe you've been hit by a run of bad luck at work and at home. Terry Apollonia, fifty-three, was just getting her life back together after her divorce when her thirty-year-old son, Tony, lost his job on Wall Street and asked if he could move back home. A year later, with Tony still out of work, Terry learned she had early-stage breast cancer and would need surgery and chemotherapy.

You have my sincere and deep sympathy for whatever pain you've experienced in the past. I may not know exactly what you've felt, but I've experienced pain and loss and sorrow, too. It was largely a childhood filled with parental pressure that helped turn me into someone who couldn't own his own success. The criticism I perceived coming from my father-in-law contributed to my becoming a workaholic. At what should have been the peak of my business career, I became ill with tuberculosis, lost my job, and had to start over again. In the past five years, I've lost my younger brother, my mother, my younger sister, and my father. I'm not trying to equate my sufferings, or those of Jimmy, Rachel, and Terry, with yours or to top your heartache. I'm just trying to point out that we have all felt pain and sorrow.

Suffering is part of the human condition. It goes hand in hand with consciousness and awareness. Let me briefly retell a famous story. There was a handsome young prince born into the royal family of the Sakyas in ancient India. So beloved was this prince that his father, the king, made sure to keep him as safe as possible. The prince was housed in a magnificent palace whose high walls kept the real world at bay. One day, the prince expressed an interest in seeing the outside world. The king made arrangements so the prince would be spared the sight of anything distressing on his trip. But by chance the prince saw an old man. He was shocked and asked about the old man. That was how he learned of pain, sorrow, disease, famine, and death. The king redoubled his efforts to keep the prince insulated from the real world, but eventually the prince escaped and began an incredible spiritual journey. The prince's name was Siddhartha, and he eventually became known as the Buddha, or the Enlightened One. The Buddha preached that all life was suffering. Practice mercy and nonviolence, defeat your passions and desires, and, the Buddha taught, suffering could be overcome. You don't have to be a Buddhist to appreciate Siddhartha's observation that suffering is the universal condition.

Thankfully, you also don't have to be the Buddha to overcome your physical suffering and be happy. All you need to do is change your attitude toward your life. Stop measuring yourself against others and accept that you're just where you're supposed to be. Stop being pessimistic about the future and instead realize that things get better. Give up being your own worst enemy and take ownership of your own success. Don't look at needing or asking for help as a sign of weakness and stop trying to go it alone. Don't wait for the best time or right time and instead realize there's no time like now, so take the action. Give up the notion that you can have everything and accept that doing your best is enough. Stop reliving and regretting your yesterdays and let the past be in the past. And don't spend your time dreaming of the future; realize tomorrow is too late.

To finally be happy, you need to accept responsibility for your own happiness. Now that you know the secrets are already inside you, all you have to do is start living them. You're not responsible for the pain and sorrow you've experienced. But you are responsible for your happiness. As the British author Allan Massie wrote, "We are responsible for actions performed in response to circumstances for which we are not responsible."

I know this is asking a lot of you. Attitudes are by their nature far more ingrained than actions. Changing how you think is a lot more difficult than changing what you do. I can't do it for you, any more than I can do it for my own loved ones. I can lead you to the precipice, but I can't take the leap of faith for you. Early in this book, I wrote that I sometimes feel like the Wizard of Oz, revealing that you hold within you that for which you've long been searching. Here, at the end of this book, I feel a bit like Moses. I've taken you right up to the border of the promised land, but I can't go there with you. You'll have to make the last leg of the journey on your own. Don't feel you need to follow my suggestions to the letter or in any particular order. The attitudes I've outlined are eight essential secrets, not eight commandments. There's no wrong way to be happy. You'll know you've reached the promised land when you wake up excited about living another day and go to sleep eager to see what the next morning will bring.

God has given us all two great gifts. The first is life itself. The second is free will. We can do with our lives what we choose. But along with that freedom comes responsibility. Eleanor Roosevelt once wrote, "Somewhere along the line of development we discover who we really are, and then we make our real decision for which we are responsible. Make that decision primarily for yourself because you can never really live anyone else's life, not even your child's. The influence you exert is through your own life and what you become yourself." It's up to you to make the decision to be happy. It's not up to your parents, your boss, your spouse, or your children. It's not even up to God. All I know is that God gave us all a chance to be happy. Who are we to turn down the gift?

Epilogue

There is that in me—I do not know what it is—but I know it
    is in me . . .
I do not know it—it is without name—it is a word unsaid,
It is not in any dictionary, utterance, symbol . . .
Do you see O my brothers and sisters?
It is not chaos or death—it is form, union, plan—it is eternal
    life—it is
Happiness.

—*Walt Whitman*

Appendix
How to Be Happy

Exercise 1

- Take out your journal and turn to a blank page.
- List all the things and activities that make you happy.
- Once you find yourself struggling to come up with more items, put your journal down for a minute.
- Close your eyes, take one deep breath, and go back and read your list.

Exercise 2

- Jealous of someone else's financial life? Take out your journal and turn to a blank page.
- Write the person's name and a characterization of their financial reward.
- Ask yourself about the risks they take to get that reward. Jot down your answer.
- Were you, or are you now, in the position to prudently take the same risk or risks?

Exercise 3

- Jealous of someone else's spouse, child, friend? Take out your journal and turn to a blank page.

- Write the name of the person in your life who you feel isn't measuring up to the complimentary person in someone else's life.
- Look at the name. Visualize the person's face. Does this person bring you joy? Does this relationship add to your life? Are you as a couple, as a family, as friends, being true to your own dynamic?

Exercise 4

- Is there an area or aspect of your life about which you're feeling negative? Take out your journal and turn to a blank page.
- Write a description of your feelings in concrete language.
- Close your eyes and give the subject a bit of thought.
- Set your journal down and do something to free up your mind.
- Return to your journal and write down as many solutions to the problem as you can come up with.
- Take each solution and, on a separate page in your journal, break it down into a series of very specific small steps.
- Repeat the process for every area of your life about which you're feeling negative.
- Decide which area you think is the most difficult to tackle.
- Turn to your pages of solutions and select the one you think is most appropriate.
- Start working on the first step you've outlined.
- When you finish with the most difficult area, start working on the next most difficult area.

Exercise 5

- Can't get out from your own head? Put yourself in situations where you're forced to face the fact that you're not the center of the universe. This could mean spending time in nature, or prayer, or exercise.
- Make this a regular part of your daily, weekly, or monthly schedule.

Exercise 6

- Think people will turn down your requests for help? Make it easier for them to say yes.
- Think about what obstacles they might face, and come up with ways to overcome those obstacles.
- Explain your request, showing why you're approaching them.
- Frame it as a specific request for help with a single problem.

Exercise 7

- Have a hard time asking for help? Practice.
- Frame all your requests for assistance, no matter how large or small, as requests for help.
- The more you "ask for help" and then receive it, without either feeling like, or being treated as, a failure, the sooner you'll internalize that it's not a big deal.

Exercise 8

- Think you can be of assistance to someone? Offer to help without waiting to be asked.
- Don't calculate if there's a possible quid pro quo—whether this person could be of assistance to you in the future.
- The more you help others, the more others will help you.

Exercise 9

- Hesitating to take on a task? Practice tackling things you fear.
- Come up with a list of actions, large and small, that you've hesitated to undertake.
- Prioritize the items by difficulty . . . and then do the most difficult one first.
- Alternatively, the moment you realize you don't want to do something, large or small, do it.
- Don't focus on the end result. Concentrate on the action itself.
- When, during the course of day-to-day life, you find yourself hesitating, or rationalizing inaction, ask what you're afraid of. Then get past your fear of failure by taking the action.

Exercise 10

- Find yourself overwhelmed with dreams? Take control of your aspirations.
- Make yourself a pot of tea or coffee, or if you prefer, pour a glass of wine. Find a comfortable, quiet place where you'll be able to sit and think for at least an hour.
- Take out your journal and turn to a blank left-hand page so you have two blank pages face-to-face.
- On top of the left-hand page write the words "The Best." On top of the right-hand page write the words "My Best."
- On the left-hand side of the left-hand page, list the important areas of your life. Skip two or three lines between each item. Once you have a list you feel confident represents most, if not all, of the important areas in your life, you can move on to the next step.
- Consider the first item on your list. What would it mean for you to be the best in that area of your life? What would it take? Write your thoughts down.
- Do this for each item on your list.
- Go over your notes. Would it be possible to achieve more than one of these goals? Or would you need to focus on just one area of your life to achieve your ultimate goal?
- Turn to the right-hand page you headed "My Best." Assume you need to incorporate all these areas into your life. What would be the minimum achievement you'd look for in each area? What would it take to achieve that minimum satisfactory goal? Write down your answers.
- Allowing for seasonal variations, resolve to set aside some time each day, or each week, to each of the areas of your life you've listed as important.
- Think of your choices as addition by subtraction.

Exercise 11

- Stop trying to forgive others and just try to let it go. Take out your journal, turn to a fresh page, and write the word "Anger" on top.

- Try to list all the grudges you are holding. Don't worry about putting them in any kind of order. Include both large and small incidents, leaving a blank space after each entry.
- Focus on the first item. In the blank space after the first entry, write down exactly what you gain by holding the grudge.
- Think about each entry and go through the same mental exercise.
- If in the future you remember further grudges, turn back to your journal, write them down, and try to come up with a benefit to holding on to your anger.

Exercise 12

- Stop trying to forgive yourself and just try to let it go. Turn to a fresh page in your journal and head it "Regret."
- Write down as many incidents as you can in which you've wronged someone in one way or another. Again, these can be large or small, from your childhood or yesterday.
- Once you've listed all the entries that come to mind right away, turn back to the first item. Come up with a way to apologize for your action or inaction.
- This might be a direct verbal apology or a mental apology during a moment of meditation.
- In cases where apologizing will do more harm than good, engage in an act of compensation.
- Having apologized for all the items you've listed in your journal, make a practice of apologizing unhesitatingly for your actions whenever it's appropriate.

Exercise 13

- Living in the future? Take out your journal and turn to a fresh page. On top of the page write the heading "Things for Which I'm Grateful."
- Start by writing, "I'm alive," and move on from there, line by line, filling as many pages as you need.
- Start by concentrating on people you love.
- Next, move on to places you love or loved.

- Finally, turn to things you value.
- On days when you're feeling down, turn back to the list you've compiled and reread what you've written. Then, after a few minutes' reflection, add some new entries to the list.

Exercise 14

- Living in the future? Tell people you're grateful for what they've done for you.
- Whenever an opportunity arises, just thank people for coming into your life.

Postscript

An Appreciation of Mark Levine

Mark Levine has been my coauthor for more than two decades. When we met, Mark was in his mid-twenties, working as the editor of a small trade journal. I, like the proverbial cat, had already lived a few of my nine lives. Mark was a quiet, gentle young man, but I could tell right away he had the goods. Little did I know that, as Bogart said to Claude Rains in *Casablanca*, "this was going to be the start of a beautiful friendship."

In the years since, we have become a real team, so much so that I can honestly say we operate symbiotically. We know each other's thoughts and can finish each other's sentences. Each of us contributes particular talents to our books in terms of research, interviewing, organization, and writing, but I know that the whole is coherent and clear because of Mark's exceptional ability to transform the dross of raw material into publishable gold. I feel as though it is Mark who has helped me to find my voice and to communicate my ideas in their most succinct and compelling form.

I have witnessed an enormous growth in Mark, from unassuming wordsmith to a geyser of knowledge. At this point in our partnership, it is much less clear who is the mentor and who is the student. I owe him an enormous dept of gratitude for our shared success. What we have aimed to do, and what I think we have achieved, has been to help our readers achieve their own best selves, and it is especially gratifying to know that in this work, I have had a collaborator who has helped me to achieve my own best self.

So with the publication of *It's All in Your Head*, our twentieth book together, I happily take this occasion to express my gratitude to Mark, the student who is fast surpassing his mentor. Neither of us could have anticipated twenty years and twenty books ago that we would end up with sailing so well-balanced a boat, through fair weather and foul. It may have helped that we each return to a different port of call, he to Ithaca and Deirdre, me to New York City and Corky.

Nor could we have guessed how the teamwork would promote an enduring affection. La Rochefoucauld said, "A true friend is the most precious of all possessions and the one we take least thought about acquiring." Well, by now I have thought about this one a lot, and take pride in calling Mark my friend and partner. And for both of these, I give deepest gratitude.

—Stephen M. Pollan

About the Authors

Stephen M. Pollan is a New York City–based attorney, financial adviser, and life strategist.

Mark Levine has been Stephen Pollan's collaborator for more than fifteen years.

Together they have authored numerous books, including the national best sellers *Lifescripts, Live Rich, Second Acts*, and *Die Broke*.